CURRICULUM AND EVALUATION

S T A N D A R D S

FOR SCHOOL MATHEMATICS

ADDENDA SERIES, GRADES K–6

N U M B E R   S E N S E   A N D   O P E R A T I O N S

Grace M. Burton

with   *Consultants*

Ann Mills   Douglas Clements

Carolyn Lennon   John Firkins

Cynthia Parker   Jeane Joyner

Miriam A. Leiva, Series Editor

NATIONAL COUNCIL OF
TEACHERS OF MATHEMATICS

Copyright © 1993 by
THE NATIONAL COUNCIL OF TEACHERS OF MATHEMATICS, INC.
1906 Association Drive, Reston, Virginia 20191-1593
All rights reserved

Fourth printing 1996

Library of Congress Cataloging-in-Publication Data:

Burton, Grace M.
  Number sense and operations / Grace Burton, with Ann Mills,
Carolyn Lennon, Cynthia Parker.
       p.   cm. — (Curriculum and evaluation standards for school
mathematics addenda series. Grades K–6)
    Includes bibliographical references.
    ISBN 0-87353-319-4
    1. Mathematics—Study and teaching (Elementary)   I. Title.
II. Series.
QA135.5.B8398   1993
372.7—dc20   92-41880
                                                              CIP

Photographs are by Patricia Fisher; artwork is by Lynn Gohman and Don Christian.

Printed in the United States of America

TABLE OF CONTENTS

FOREWORD

The *Curriculum and Evaluation Standards for School Mathematics* (NCTM 1989a) describes a framework for revising and strengthening school mathematics. This visionary document provides a set of guidelines for K–12 mathematics curricula and for evaluating both the mathematics curriculum and students' progress. It addresses not only what mathematics students should learn but also how they should learn it.

As the document was being developed, it became apparent that supporting publications would be needed to interpret and illustrate how the vision could be translated realistically into classroom practices. A Task Force on the Addenda to the *Curriculum and Evaluation Standards for School Mathematics,* chaired by Thomas Rowan and composed of Joan Duea, Christian Hirsch, Marie Jernigan, and Richard Lodholz, was appointed by Shirley Frye, then NCTM president. The Task Force's recommendations on the scope and nature of the supporting publications were submitted to the Educational Materials Committee, which subsequently framed the Addenda Project.

Central to the Addenda Project was the formation of three writing teams—consisting of classroom teachers, mathematics supervisors, and university mathematics educators—to prepare a series of publications, the Addenda Series, targeted at mathematics instruction in grades K–6, 5–8, and 9–12. The purpose of the series is to clarify and illustrate the message of the *Curriculum and Evaluation Standards.* The underlying themes of problem solving, reasoning, communication, and connections are woven throughout the materials, as is the view of assessment as a means of guiding instruction. Activities have been field-tested by teachers to ensure that they reflect the realities of today's classrooms.

It is envisioned that the Addenda Series will be a source of ideas by teachers as they begin to implement the recommendations in the NCTM *Curriculum and Evaluation Standards.* Individual volumes in the series are appropriate for in-service programs and for preservice courses in teacher education programs.

A project of this magnitude required the efforts and talents of many people over an extended time. Two NCTM presidents, Shirley Frye and Iris Carl, supported and inspired these efforts. A third president, Mary Lindquist, gave countless hours and creative energy to the project. The Addenda Series is a tribute to them. Sincerest appreciation is extended to the elementary school teachers throughout the United States and Canada who played key roles in developing, revising, and trying out the materials for the Number Sense and Operations book. The K–6 writing team and consultants Grace Burton, Douglas Clements, Terrence Coburn, John Del Grande, John Firkins, Jeane Joyner, Mary M. Lindquist, and Lorna Morrow are thanked for their collaboration and contributions to all the books in the series. A special word of gratitude is given to Holly Baker of the NCTM publications staff for her outstanding and sensitive editorial work and her commitment to excellence in producing the Addenda Series. Finally, this project would not have materialized without the outstanding technical support supplied by Cynthia Rosso and the NCTM publications staff.

Bonnie H. Litwiller
Addenda Project Coordinator

PREFACE

Something exciting is happening in many elementary school classrooms! A vision of an innovative mathematics program is coming alive. There *is* a shift in emphasis in the teaching and learning of mathematics. Teachers are encouraging children to investigate, discuss, question, and verify. They are focusing on explorations and dialogues. They are using various strategies to assess students' progress. They are making mathematics accessible to all children while exposing them to the value and the beauty of mathematics. Teachers and students are excited, and their enthusiasm is contagious. You can *catch it* when you hear children confidently explaining their solutions to the class, when you see them modeling problems with manipulatives, and when you observe them using a variety of methods and materials to arrive at answers. Some children are working with paper and pencil or with calculators; others are sharpening their estimation and mental math skills. There is noise in these classrooms—the sounds of students actively participating in the class and constructing their own knowledge through experiences that will give them confidence in their own abilities and make them mathematically powerful.

We must go beyond how we were taught and teach how we wish we had been taught. We must bring to life a vision of what a mathematics classroom should be.

Rationale for Change

These are challenging times for you, the teachers of elementary school mathematics, and for your students. Major reforms in school mathematics are advocated in reports that call for changes in the curriculum, in student and program evaluations, in instruction, and in the classroom environment.

The blueprint for reform is the *Curriculum and Evaluation Standards for School Mathematics* (National Council of Teachers of Mathematics 1989a), which identifies a set of standards for the mathematics curriculum in grades K–12 as well as standards for evaluating the quality of programs and students' performance. The *Curriculum and Evaluation Standards* sets forth a bold vision of what mathematics education in grades K–12 should be and describes how mathematics classrooms can fit the vision.

Mathematics as Sense Making

In the past, mathematics classrooms were dominated by instruction and performance of rote procedures "to get the right answer." The *Curriculum and Evaluation Standards* supports the view of school mathematics as a sense-making experience encompassing a wide range of content, instructional approaches, and evaluation techniques.

Four standards are closely woven into content and instruction: mathematics as problem solving, mathematics as communication, mathematics as reasoning, and mathematical connections. These strands are common themes that support all other standards throughout all grade levels.

A primary goal for the study of mathematics is to give children experiences that promote the ability *to solve problems* and that build mathematics from situations generated within the context of everyday experiences. Students are also expected *to make conjectures and conclusions* and *to discuss their reasoning* in words, both written and spoken; with pictures, graphs, and charts; and with manipulatives. Moreover, students learn *to value mathematics* when they *make connections* between

"I covered the apple with 7 square tiles and Carlos covered his with 12 goldfish crackers."

topics in mathematics, between the concrete and the abstract, between concepts and skills, and between mathematics and other areas in the curriculum.

The Changing Roles of Students

Previous efforts to reform school mathematics focused primarily on the curriculum; the *Curriculum and Evaluation Standards* also deals with other factors—in particular, students—that affect and are affected by reforms. The role of students is redirected from passive recipients to active participants, from isolated workers to team members, from listeners to investigators and reporters, and from timid followers to intrepid explorers and risk takers. They are asked to develop, discuss, create, model, validate, and investigate to learn mathematics.

Many people, including students, believe that mathematics is for the privileged few. It is time to dispel that myth. All children, regardless of sex, socioeconomic background, language, race, or ethnic origin, can and must succeed in school mathematics. With proper instruction, encouragement, and high expectations, *all* students can do mathematics.

Your Role in Implementing the Standards

All elementary school teachers are teachers of mathematics. Thus, your role is to build your students' self-confidence and nurture their natural curiosity; to challenge them with rich problems through which they will learn to value mathematics and appreciate the order and beauty of mathematics; to provide them with a strong foundation for further study; and to encourage their mathematical ability and power.

The elementary school years are crucial in a child's cognitive and affective development, and you are the central figure. You structure classroom experiences to implement the curriculum and create a supportive environment for learning to take place. You are the guide, the coach, the facilitator, and the instigator of mathematical explorations.

Implementing the Evaluation Standards

Evaluation must be an integral part of teaching. A primary component of instruction is an ongoing assessment of what goes on in our classrooms. This information helps us make decisions about what we teach and how we teach it, about students' progress and feelings, and about our mathematics program.

The *Curriculum and Evaluation Standards* advocates many changes in curriculum, in instruction, and in the roles of students and teachers. None of these changes are more important than those related to evaluation. We must learn to use a variety of assessment instruments and not depend on pencil-and-paper tests alone. Tools such as observations, interviews, projects, reports, portfolios, diaries, and tests provide a more complete picture of what children understand and are able to use. Knowing what questions to ask is a skill we must develop.

When we test, we send a message about what we think is important. Because we encourage reasoning and communicating mathematically, we practice these skills. Because manipulatives and calculators are valuable tools for learning, we promote their use in the classroom. Because we want children to experience cooperative problem solving, we provide opportunities for group activities. *We must evaluate not only what we want children to learn, but also how we want them to learn it.*

"*My goal is to give all my students the opportunity to succeed in mathematics and to develop the unique talents each of them possesses.*"

"*My mom thought that we popped corn just for fun, until I showed her the story I wrote about how we guessed and measured in math class.*"

You and This Book

This book is part of the *Curriculum and Evaluation for School Mathematics* Addenda Series, Grades K–6. This series was designed to illustrate the standards and to help you translate them into classroom practice.

In this book, *Number Sense and Operations,* both traditional and new topics are explored in chapters labeled Kindergarten through Sixth Grade. The grade level distinctions are merely suggestions; you are invited to peruse the entire document for activities appropriate for your class. You are encouraged to extend or adapt these lessons to your students and their needs. The mathematical topics presented in this booklet support the development of both number sense and operation sense described in the *Curriculum and Evaluation Standards for School Mathematics* (NCTM 1989). Appropriate mathematical tasks, classroom discourse, pedagogical strategies, learning environments, and teaching and learning considerations have also been informed by the *Professional Standards for Teaching Mathematics* (NCTM 1991).

In *Number Sense and Operations,* you will find that familiar activities have been redesigned and infused with an investigative flavor. You will also discover new ideas that can be easily incorporated into your mathematics program. You will also encounter a variety of problems and questions to explore with your class. Margin notes give you additional information on the activities and on such topics as student self-confidence, evaluation, and grouping. Connections to science, language arts, social studies, and other areas in the curriculum are made throughout. Supporting statements from the *Curriculum and Evaluation Standards* appear as margin notes.

Change is an ongoing process that takes time and courage. It is not easy to go beyond comfort and security to try new things. As you use this book, pick and choose at will, and sample alternative approaches and ideas for instruction and assessment. Savor the freedom of change. All the documents in the world will not effect change in the classrooms; *only you can.*

The Challenge and the Vision

"I wonder why...?"
"What would happen if ...?"
"Can you do it another way?"

"Why do you think that's so?"
"Tell me about your pattern."
"Our group has a different solution."

These inviting words give students the freedom to be creative, the confidence to solve problems, and the power to do mathematics. When you give your students the opportunity to construct their own knowledge, you are opening the doors of mathematics to *all* young learners.

This is the challenge. This is the vision.

Miriam A. Leiva, Editor
K–6 Addenda Series

"I listen to my students talk to each other during group work. It helps me evaluate their work and the lesson."

"When my sixth-grade students had the unit on population density we studied area, growth rate, projected population, and the use of census data. It gave me a good opportunity to make connections within mathematics and with social studies."

I love math. It's the best part of the day.

BIBLIOGRAPHY

Baratta-Lorton, Mary. *Mathematics Their Way.* Menlo Park, Calif.: Addison-Wesley Publishing Co., 1976.

————. *Workjobs II.* Menlo Park, Calif.: Addison-Wesley Publishing Co., 1976.

National Council of Teachers of Mathematics. *Curriculum and Evaluation Standards for School Mathematics* Addenda Series, Grades K–6, edited by Miriam A. Leiva. Reston, Va.: The Council, 1991.

————. *Curriculum and Evaluation Standards for School Mathematics* Addenda Series, Grades 5–8, edited by Frances R. Curcio. Reston, Va.: The Council, 1991–92.

————. *Curriculum and Evaluation Standards for School Mathematics* Addenda Series, Grades 9–12, edited by Christian R. Hirsch. Reston, Va.: The Council, 1991–92.

————. *Curriculum and Evaluation Standards for School Mathematics.* Reston, Va.: The Council, 1989a.

————. *New Directions for Elementary School Mathematics.* 1989 Yearbook of the National Council of Teachers of Mathematics, edited by Paul Trafton. Reston, Va.: The Council, 1989b.

————. *Professional Standards for Teaching Mathematics.* Reston, Va.: The Council, 1991.

National Research Council. *Everybody Counts: A Report to the Nation on the Future of Mathematics Education.* Washington, D.C.: National Academy Press, 1989.

Wirtz, Robert. *Drill and Practice at the Problem Solving Level.* Washington, D.C.: Curriculum Development Associates, 1974.

ACKNOWLEDGMENTS

In his classic *Zen and the Art of Motorcycle Maintenance,* Robert Pirsig says, "The place to improve the world is first in one's own heart and head and hands, and to work outward from there." It is only when dedicated professionals are willing to make such changes that progress, in mathematics education or in any other endeavor, happens. The material that you will find in this booklet is the result of such considered changes on the part of many people, but particularly three gifted teachers from the New Hanover County school system in Wilmington, North Carolina. They deserve more than just this public thanks for their efforts. To Ann Mills, Carolyn Lennon, and Cynthia Parker—thank you for your desire to help each child succeed, for your careful study of how children learn mathematics best, and for your willingness to work above and beyond the call of duty to facilitate change.

My sincere appreciation, too, goes to the other members of the Grades K–6 Addenda writing team for their constant vigilance and encouragement and for their good ideas and good humor. A most special thank you goes to Miriam Leiva, the series editor, who supplied her writing team with chocolates and copious correspondence and with phone calls and pats on the back far surpassing what we could have reasonably expected.

It has been a joy to work with you all.

Grace M. Burton, Author
Number Sense and Operations

INTRODUCTION

When we say that someone has good number sense, we mean that he or she possesses a variety of abilities and understandings that include an awareness of the relationships between numbers, an ability to represent numbers in a variety of ways, a knowledge of the effects of operations, and an ability to interpret and use numbers in real-world counting and measurement situations. Such a person predicts with some accuracy the result of an operation and consistently chooses appropriate measurement units. This "friendliness with numbers" goes far beyond mere memorization of computational algorithms and number facts; it implies an ability to use numbers flexibly, to choose the most appropriate representation of a number for a given circumstance, and to recognize when operations have been correctly performed.

Seasoned teachers will attest to the fact that, given a mathematical question, some students unabashedly give answers that are obviously far from correct. Giving 114, for example, as the product of 38 and 0.3, or reporting that bananas cost .33 cents a pound, seems not to bother them at all—despite the fact that they are aware that a pencil-and-paper algorithm would result in a radically different answer or that their answer is not congruent with what they know about the real world. Such students either do not possess, or are not using, number sense. It is not that they do not know the number combinations or cannot execute algorithms; it is more likely that they have neither accurately predicted what the answer might be nor compared their prediction with the computation result.

Students with number sense pay attention to the meaning of numbers and operations and make realistic estimates of the results of computation. They can discuss which size unit will be convenient to use when measurements are to be taken, and they seem to be intuitively aware when an answer is "out of the ballpark." These abilities to deal sensibly with numbers stand students in good stead both in and out of the classroom.

Students who have number sense possess an accurate notion of how numbers relate to each other and how they provide information about the real world. By observing children and listening to their informal conversations, teachers are able to gather information about the extent to which number sense ability is characteristic of each individual student. By continually assessing the children's levels of understanding and using that information to structure a variety of positive experiences, you will be able to enhance each child's feelings of mathematical competence.

Developing a sense of number begins informally before children enter school and in a focused manner during kindergarten; the process continues throughout the elementary school years, and even beyond, and evolves from the total classroom experience as well as through specific activities. Students develop a solid understanding of number when teachers call attention to the many ways numbers are used in everyday life, provide opportunities for children to explore number relationships with different objects, and encourage conversations about these concepts. When children count things in the classroom or begin to explore the operations of addition or subtraction, they are extending their earlier ideas of number. When they organize and compare groups of objects and examine multiple representations of the same numbers, they continue to broaden their understandings. These new ideas about number

Intuition about number relationships helps children make judgments about the reasonableness of computational results and of proposed solutions to numerical problems. (NCTM 1989a, p. 38)

Students need to see when and how mathematics can be used, rather than to be promised that someday they will use it. (NCTM 1989a, p.35)

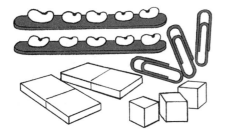

relationships provide a foundation for understanding number magnitude and the effects of arithmetic operations.

The same is true in real-world applications of number. Children's early experiences in measurement pave the way for more formal experiences later. Given an opportunity to explore and experiment, children demonstrate an increasing ability to use measurement ideas in and out of school. If a child has number sense with respect to measurement, he or she understands the relationship among units, is able to tell when using a particular unit is reasonable, uses estimation when appropriate, and can measure accurately and precisely in many situations. These abilities are nurtured when teachers provide students with interesting measurement questions to explore, suitable materials with which to investigate those questions, and a time and a place to discuss and display the results of their investigations.

Number sense, as a topic, has not been a part of the traditional mathematics curriculum, but this should not hinder today's teachers from making it an important component of contemporary school mathematics. To help students develop this very valuable ability, teachers can provide children with experiences that encourage them to model and describe numbers in many ways and to apply mathematics understandings in appropriate and efficient ways. Encouraging students to estimate answers, making checking computation an integral part of any numerical exercise, discussing common measurement situations, and asking students to justify mathematical choices will help students develop this crucial ability. It would be best if such experiences were part of the curriculum from kindergarten on, but it is never too late to begin.

When many of us were in school, doing mathematics was a silent pencil-and-paper occupation. Although we may have participated in mathematics quite passively, a vast body of research has shown that children learn best when they are active learners, trying new ways to find answers to problems and talking with their classmates about what they are learning. Research also indicates that pencil-and-paper activities should follow extensive exploration of numerical relationships with manipulatives. Many different materials can be used in these mathematical investigations: beans glued onto craft or ice pop sticks, dominoes, paper clips, small cubes, or just about any other easily handled item. Computers and calculators, pencil and paper, prepared worksheets, and student textbooks also have a place in the investigations appropriate in the modern elementary school mathematics classroom.

Since understandings about numbers develop best in situations that have meaning to children, those requiring the use of number sense must be an on-going feature of classroom routines from the first days of school. At the kindergarten level, for example, children can be given directions that require using number in various settings, such as limiting the number of children allowed in the art center to five, asking children to distribute supplies one to each child, giving directions such as "the second person in line may hold the door," and requiring that supplies be counted as they are given out or put away.

Children in grades 1 through 3 also need to develop an increasing awareness of the many ways number and measurement are used in everyday life and in the possible multiple representations of number. These concepts can be integrated into the normal classroom routine by having students develop their own algorithms using base ten materials, suggesting that students measure themselves and their belongings with a wide variety of nonstandard measuring devices, and providing opportunities for estimation and verification of quantities, lengths, and weights on a continuing basis.

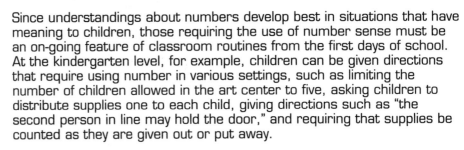

In fourth through sixth grade, students typically begin a more intensive study of rational numbers. Extending their understanding of whole numbers becomes a major focus. Students at this level who possess number sense typically use their skills appropriately in a variety of settings inside and outside the classroom and use mathematical reasoning to justify their results. They enjoy working together or alone to investigate puzzling events and solve problems. Activities that capitalize on this curiosity motivate students to explore mathematical questions and to make and verify predictions.

A student with number sense understands both the relationships between numbers and the effects of operations on numbers. Since this aspect of number sense develops slowly over many years and is very dependent on the experiences a child has had, there may be a wide disparity among the concepts and skills of students, especially at the upper grade levels. Whatever concepts and skills they possess, will be fostered in an environment in which students are encouraged to discuss the findings of their investigations and to apply them to other situations. Activities that allow the students a chance to pose and solve interesting questions dealing with number and measurement must be an integral part of the elementary school mathematics curriculum. Some activities for various grade levels are presented on the following pages. These are suggestions only; you are the best judge of how to adapt them to best fit your class.

Our vision sees teachers encouraging students' probing for ideas, and carefully judging the maturity of a student's thoughts and expressions. (NCTM 1989a, p. 10)

CHAPTER 1
KINDERGARTEN

Counting skills, which are essential for ordering and comparing numbers, are an important component of the development of number ideas. Counting on, counting back, and skip counting mark advances in children's development of number ideas. However, counting is only one indicator of children's understanding of numbers. (NCTM 1989a, p. 39)

In kindergarten, number sense evolves from the total classroom experience as well as through specific activities. If we want children to develop a solid understanding of numerical concepts, we must call attention to the many ways numbers are used in everyday life, provide opportunities for children to explore number relationships with different objects, and encourage conversations about these concepts.

Although developing a sense of number begins before children enter school and continues in a focused manner throughout kindergarten, the process is long and takes many years. This chapter focuses on developing number sense through dramatizations, rote counting, estimating "how many," counting objects, and using numbers in playing games.

WE CAN DO IT!

Get ready. The purposes of this activity are to reinforce ordinal and cardinal numbers and to help children visualize the effects of adding to the group or removing from the group.

You will want to use many different finger plays throughout the year, varying the topics with the season.

Get going. Tell the children that instead of using their fingers to tell the story of the five little pumpkins, the class will act out the finger play. Children will take turns acting out the rhyme while the entire class tells the story.

> Five little pumpkins are sitting on a gate.
> *(Five children sit on chairs or the floor.)*
>
> The first one said, "Oh my, it's getting late."
> *(The first pumpkin stands, says the line, and then sits.)*
>
> The second one said, "There are witches in the air."
> *(The second child stands for the line and then sits down as the third child speaks.)*
>
> The third one said, "But we don't care!"
> *(The third child does the same.)*
>
> The fourth one said, "Let's run and run and run."
> *(The fourth pumpkin speaks with enthusiasm.)*
>
> The fifth one said, "I'm ready for some fun!"
> *(The fifth pumpkin stands to tell the class.)*
>
> "Whooo-oo-oo" went the wind and out went the lights!
> *(All children tell the story from their seats.)*
>
> And the five little pumpkins rolled out of sight.
> *(Pumpkins scurry off the stage.)*

Have the children return to their places "on the gate" and ask them to tell about the story:

What happened first in the story?

Who is the first pumpkin? Who is the fourth pumpkin?

Who comes next after the second pumpkin?

Some Ways to Develop Number Sense

♦ *Sorting and classifying*

♦ *Comparing and ordering*

♦ *Using 1-to-1 correspondence*

♦ *Counting objects*

♦ *Using numbers—for example, in playing games*

♦ *Talking about numbers in daily life*

♦ *Solving problems involving numbers in varied ways and discussing the solution strategies*

The last pumpkin is in which place?

When all five pumpkins ran away, how many were left sitting on the gate? What number means "not any"?

How many children will we need to choose if we say the poem again and there are different "pumpkins"?

Counting backward is good preparation for subtraction. Children may enjoy counting down using a calculator while the rhyme is recited.

Activities that use mathematics in other subject areas enhance the curriculum. This activity makes connections with language arts as students discuss their experiences using mathematical concepts.

Because other children will want a turn being the pumpkins, repeat the poem several times. You might allow the children to choose their own replacements:

John, please choose someone to be the first pumpkin.

On other occasions you can designate the "pumpkins" and ask the students different questions as a part of the process:

We have three pumpkins for the play. How many more do I need to choose?

Jackie is the second pumpkin. Which one will come next?

You might also wish to have the children decorate with faces five orange cardboard disks or five lima beans spray-painted orange. Each child can then act out the story line with his or her own set of pumpkins.

Keep going. Many finger plays practice rote counting, both forward and backward. Others, such as "Ten Little Monkeys," allow children to observe counting backward or subtraction situations. Because shy children will sometimes role play more readily than they will answer questions, dramatization fosters their language development while they talk about mathematics.

Ten Little Monkeys

Ten little monkeys jumping on the bed.

One fell off and broke his head.

Called for the doctor and the doctor said,

"No more monkeys jumping on the bed!"

Repeat the rhyme for nine little monkeys and so on, down to one little monkey.

SHOW ME ON TEDDY'S MAT

Get ready. The purposes of this activity are to have the children count objects and compare sets. Each pair of children needs a copy of Teddy's Mat and counters (see page 9).

When children work together on a problem, they have a chance to justify their choices and to consider the reasoning patterns of their partner. Realizing there is more than one way to arrive at an answer is an important step toward mathematical maturity.

Get going. Ask the first partner to place two counters on one side of Teddy's Mat while counting aloud. Tell the second partner to put three counters on the other side of the mat.

Which side has more? Show me how you know.

Repeat the activity, using different numbers. Allow different children to tell about the counters, and continue to ask questions:

The first person has five counters. What number could the second person place on the other side so that there would be fewer? If you put seven counters on the other side, would that be more or fewer than five?

If we want to have the same number of counters on each side, who can tell what we might do?

Keep going. Use this activity as a mathematics learning center game by having the children take turns rolling a die and placing that many counters on their side of Teddy's Mat. The children then compare to see who has more counters, fewer counters, or the same number of counters.

If appropriate, have the students match the correct numerals with their sets. Also, ask them to compare the sets and to think about how many more the person with fewer counters would need so that there would be the same number of counters on both sides of the mat.

For a variation use blocks of the same size and weight. Have each child roll a number cube and make a group of that number of blocks.

Which group of blocks do you think weighs more? (Have children put them on a balance scale to check.)

How many blocks should we add to one side to make the groups balance?

Is there any other way to make the groups balance?

You have eight blocks altogether. Could you split them into different groups? What do you think will happen when you put the new groups on the balance?

TEDDY BEAR'S TRIP

Get ready. The purpose of this activity is to have children use logical thinking and counting in a game situation.

Children may play in groups of two, three, or four, with each child seated on one side of a Teddy Bear's Board work mat (see page 10). They will need one work mat for the group and a teddy bear counter (or a teddy bear cracker) for each child, preferably in different colors.

Get going. To begin, the children place their bears at any point along the edges of the work mat. The children take turns rolling a number cube (or using a spinner) and moving their bear that number of spaces in one direction. Bears may be moved in any direction. They also may be moved fewer spaces than the number rolled, but they can only go in one direction on each turn. When a player comes to a fence, the bear must stop, since it cannot cross over fences. The goal is to move from one striped edge to the other striped edge or from one wavy edge to the other wavy edge.

The play continues until all bears have reached the opposite side of the board. Encourage the children to talk about different ways to move at their turns:

Are some moves better than others? Why?

Keep going. Moving across the work mat lets the children practice matching the number of spaces moved to the number rolled or to a lesser number. Deciding what to do develops logical thinking. As the

When introducing a new game, play with the children to establish clearly the rules and the purpose of the game.

Game boards with other "fences" can be made to provide other problem-solving situations.

Several computer programs offer similar games. Children can play at different ability levels and are encouraged to invent mathematical strategies.

students become more independent, have them try to move their markers to one side before their opponents reach the opposite side.

DOMINO BEARS

Get ready. The purpose of these activities is to develop children's counting and matching abilities. In the first activity each child needs a copy of Teddy's Mat; in subsequent activities children work in pairs and each pair of children needs one copy of Teddy's Mat and a set of double-six dominoes.

Get going. To begin, have the children place the dominoes face down on the table or the floor. Note that in some activities the dominoes are viewed as having two separate numbers. In others the total number of dots is used.

Match It

Each child draws one domino and places counters on Teddy's Mat to duplicate the domino. If appropriate, the child should match a numeral card to each side. The students tell their partners about the domino on the mat.

Doubles Search

The children take turns turning up one domino at a time. If the domino is a double, the children may place it on their side of Teddy's Mat by explaining to their partner how they know it is a double. If the domino is not a double, it is placed in the discard pile. The object of the game is to collect the most doubles. A more challenging activity is to have the students search for and keep dominoes that have either a four or a five on them.

Seven Out

The children take turns turning up one domino at a time and counting the dots. If the domino has a total of seven dots, it must be discarded. If the domino has any number other than seven dots, the children may claim it for their side of the board by explaining why the domino has more or fewer than seven dots. When all dominoes have been examined, the winner is the child with the most dominoes.

Who Has More?

Two children draw dominoes simultaneously. They place their domino on their side of Teddy's Mat. The child with the most dots wins the round and claims both dominoes. Play continues until all dominoes are drawn. The child with the most dominoes wins the game.

Target

Each student draws one card from a deck containing cards numbered 4, 5, 6, 7, and 8. This number is the child's special "target" for the game. The children take turns picking up a domino. If the domino has a total number of dots equal to or greater than the target number, the student keeps the domino. If not, the domino is discarded. When all dominoes have been examined, the children with two or more dominoes win.

Keep going. Make "yummy dominoes." Place three or four dominoes in the art center. The children duplicate their favorite domino by placing raisins on graham crackers, using peanut butter as the glue. The children may cover the entire graham cracker with peanut butter and place

the raisins appropriately or use dots of peanut butter to stick individual raisins to the cracker.

As an extension, have children replicate their favorite domino on an index card. The index cards can then be grouped to make a graph showing the favorite dominoes. You may wish to let the children eat their domino snack as they discuss the graph.

Have children print their names on their domino cards before making the graph about Our Favorite Dominoes.

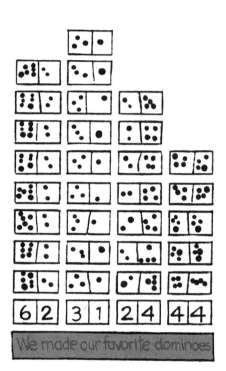

TEDDY'S MAT

TEDDY BEAR'S BOARD

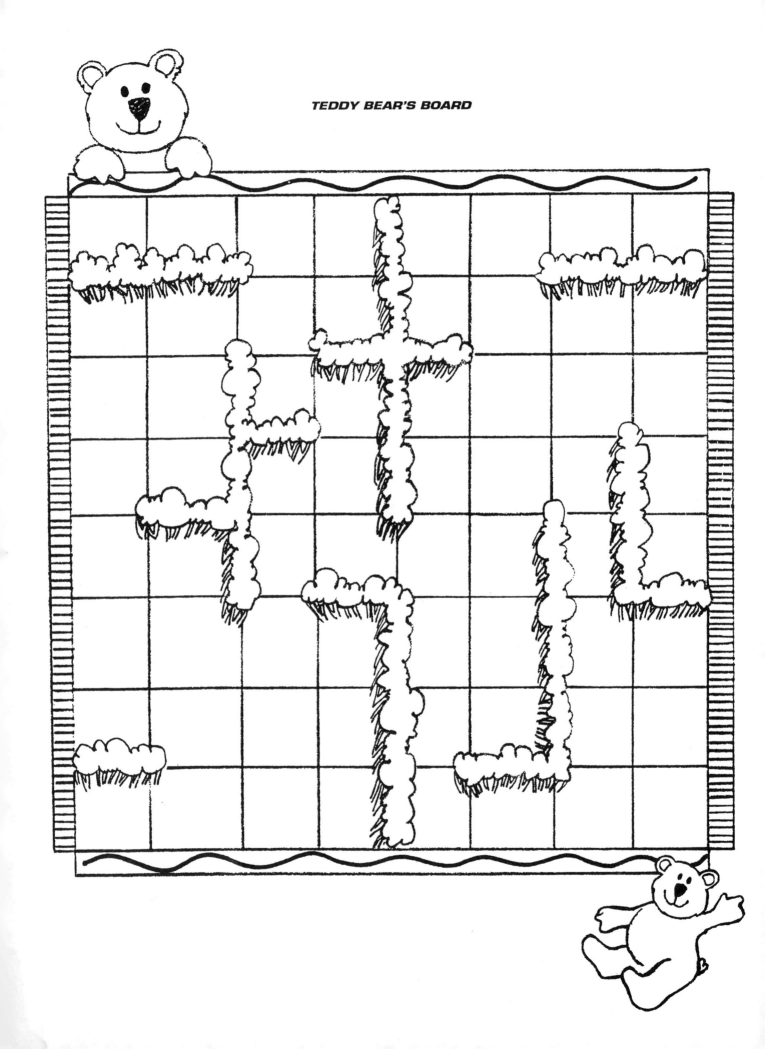

CHAPTER 2
FIRST GRADE

Children need to be encouraged to talk and write about what they have learned, and pencil-and-paper activities should follow extensive exploration of numerical relationships with manipulatives. In the following set of activities, children use materials, such as beans and dominos, to investigate ideas about number. Because the children are learning through active involvement with manipulatives, they will be better able to demonstrate and communicate their knowledge.

To illustrate for parents how children are using these materials to learn mathematical concepts, you might send them a special newsletter, have a family mathematics night program, or create a special mathematics display for an open house. Children can make many samples for their parents to enjoy. For example, have children glue toothpicks on a file card and use numbers to describe the designs in various ways.

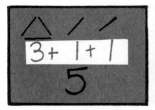 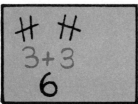 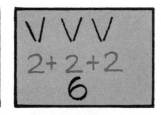

The activities with the computer using the Logo programming language furnish opportunities for linking concrete experiences with more abstract mathematics. Such bridges help students understand the concepts involved. They also help students appreciate the connections between what they study in school and the multiple uses of numbers in the world.

LADYBUGS AND LEAVES

Get ready. The purpose of this activity is to have children investigate the different ways a number can be expressed as the sum of two addends.

Use the blackline master on page 16 to make a work mat for each child. Each child also needs ten beans, which can be painted to look like ladybugs. To make ladybugs, spray-paint lima beans red and dot them with a permanent marker to make the spots. You may also use red cubes or other counters as ladybugs.

Get going. Distribute the work mats and the ladybugs. Plan time for the children to play with their materials. Suggest that they make up stories to act out for each other.

Bring the group together by telling the children a story that you have made up about six ladybugs. Ask them to model your story by putting three ladybugs on each leaf and putting the rest of their ladybugs away.

Can you put the ladybugs on the leaves in another way? How many different arrangements can you find? (Consider 1 + 5 and 5 + 1 as different arrangements.)

Record the children's findings on the chalkboard. If the children suggest

Children must understand numbers if they are to make sense of the ways numbers are used in their everyday world. (NCTM 1989a, p. 38)

A first-grade teacher relates, "Yesterday my lesson was on estimation and how to make a smart guess. The kids enjoyed guessing my age. I had guesses between 19 and 88! Then I gave them clues like 'My grandmother is 81 and my mom is 46.' You could see the wheels turning. Finally someone guessed 26! I am always nervous when someone asks me to estimate. I can't remember estimating when I was in school. I'm glad things have changed."

A rich understanding of number forms the basis for counting, arithmetic, and real-world applications. Children need experiences with manipulatives to develop number sense—paper-and-pencil work alone is not sufficient for most children.

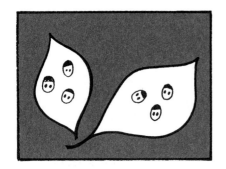

Organizing the number sentences in a structured format helps students find all the combinations and discover the resulting patterns.

$$6 + 0 = 6$$
$$5 + 1 = 6$$
$$4 + 2 = 6$$
$$3 + 3 = 6$$
$$2 + 4 = 6$$
$$1 + 5 = 6$$
$$0 + 6 = 6$$

Number of ladybugs	Ways to arrange ladybugs
3	4
4	5
5	?
6	?

arrangements in random order, talk with them about ways to organize the list.

Challenge them to find and record all possible arrangements. Have them work in pairs to decide if they have found all possible combinations. After they have written the combinations and organized the data, encourage them to find the patterns that emerge. For example, students may notice that as the first number (addend) gets smaller by 1, the second number (addend) gets larger by 1. Others may say that the answer (sum) is always 6.

Keep going. Ask the children if they can predict the number of possible arrangements for different numbers of ladybugs.

Do you think that larger numbers have more arrangements than smaller numbers? How could we find out? Let's try it with three ladybugs. How many ways can you arrange them? Now try four ladybugs.

Show students how to make a chart for recording their findings when they experiment with the ladybugs on the work mats.

How many arrangements are there for five? For six? For seven?

Can you predict how many there will be for eight? For twenty-two? How did you figure that out?

The ladybugs can also be used for a variety of other explorations, such as the following readiness activity for missing addend and comparison subtraction problems. Give the children ten ladybugs and a work mat. Ask them to place four ladybugs on one leaf. Then ask,

How many will be on the other leaf?

If you have eight ladybugs altogether and three of them are on one leaf, how many are on the other leaf?

Let the children explore missing addends and comparisons with other numbers and discuss their strategies for solving the problems. For example, you might say,

If there are six ladybugs on one leaf and nine on the other, how many more ladybugs are there on the second leaf?

HOW MANY LADYBUGS?

Get ready. The purpose of this activity is to give children opportunities to estimate, count, and group objects. Complete this investigation with the class before children work independently on similar tasks.

Use the ladybugs and the leaf work mat from the previous lesson. Have the children work in pairs. Give a recording sheet to each pair of children.

Get going. Ask each pair of students to estimate the number of ladybugs needed to cover the smaller leaf. Have them talk about their answer and write down their mutual estimate. Tell the students to cover the smaller leaf with ladybugs.

When we cover our leaves, do you think all of us will use the same number of ladybugs for the smaller leaf? Why or why not?

How many ladybugs did you use? Is that more or fewer than you

guessed? Would it take more or fewer ladybugs if you used very large ones to cover your leaves?

Have the children record their count and repeat the activity by estimating how many ladybugs it will take to cover the other leaf, recording their estimate, covering the second figure, counting the number of ladybugs, and recording the actual count.

Was your estimate for the second leaf closer than your first estimate? Why do you think this happened?

Keep going. Ask the students to group the ladybugs by fives.

If you count them by fives, do you think you will have the same total that you had when you counted by ones?

Have the children experiment with grouping the ladybugs and counting by twos and tens.

Because children learn through multiple experiences and enjoy similar activities using different materials, you may want to repeat these lessons with other manipulatives. Instead of ladybugs and leaves, you might try blocks in two boxes or paper fish in two ponds. Using animal-shaped cereal as counters appeals to children, especially when the children are allowed to eat the manipulatives at the end of the lesson. Directions may be written on task cards to make the activity appropriate for an independent center.

One way to assess a child's understanding of the number relationships explored in these activities is to present a new material, such as interlocking cubes, and ask the child to demonstrate several ways a given number, such as 5, can be shown.

This activity makes connections between counting, developing patterns, and organizing data.

DOMINO FUN

Get ready. The purpose of this activity is to have children develop an understanding of number relationships and of ordering numbers. Have the students work in pairs, sharing a set of dominoes; each child will need a copy of the blackline master Domino Record Sheet (p. 16).

Get going. Hold up a domino and have the children tell the total number of dots. Then ask them to find a domino that has more dots and to find another that has fewer dots.

Hold up a domino and ask the children to find a domino that has one dot more and to find another that has one dot less.

Did all of you find the same domino? How are they different? How are they all the same?

Is there a domino for which you cannot find another domino with more dots? With fewer dots?

I am thinking of a domino that has five dots. What could it look like? Record the possibilities on the board.

How many dots would the domino have if it had one more dot? What would it look like? Is there more than one answer?

I have another domino. If you added one more dot, there would be eight dots altogether. What domino could I have? Draw the possibilities as students suggest the various dominoes that have seven dots.

Give the students a copy of the blackline master. Demonstrate how to draw a domino and record the solutions. Notice that the blackline master, with your modifications, can be used in a variety of ways, some very structured and others more open-ended.

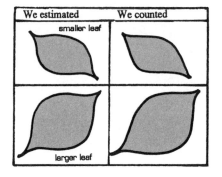

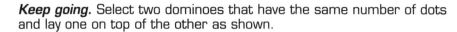

$$7 = 4 + \boxed{} \qquad 4 + \boxed{} = 7$$

"There are seven dots on my top domino. I can see four on the bottom, so there must be three hidden."

Some children may point to an imaginary path on the floor; others may describe it orally; and still others might draw a representation on the chalkboard.

Keep going. Select two dominoes that have the same number of dots and lay one on top of the other as shown.

If you know that both dominoes have the same number of dots, how many dots must be covered up?

How many different problems could we make with these two dominoes by covering up different parts?

STEPPING

Get ready. The purposes of this activity are to have children follow directions, estimate, measure and describe geometric paths, and carry out a computer algorithm.

Children will need a copy of the blackline master Turtle Time (p. 17) and access to a computer. A computer with a large screen or a display unit for use with an overhead projector is ideal for whole-class computer work, although first graders willingly gather around a small screen.

Get going. Ask the class, *How many heel-to-toe steps do you think it would take to go across the classroom?* Record their estimates and have the children check their guesses by walking. Repeat with other distances and locations.

Everyone stand up and spread out. Guess where you would be if you walked forward eight steps. Try it.

Imagine you are at a street corner and want to make a right turn. Point in the direction you would be facing. Go ahead and turn right. Turn right again. Once more. How many right turns did it take to turn all the way around?

Give other similar directions; include left turns, turning halfway around, and so on.

Face me. Guess where you would be if you walked forward five steps, turned right, and walked forward five steps again. Try it.

If you had been walking in the sand, what path would your footprints have left? Have the students describe and draw this path. Repeat with other directions.

Write the following directions on the chalkboard or an overhead transparency:

1. Mark a starting place.
2. Take 6 heel-and-toe steps forward.
3. Turn right.
4. Walk forward 8 heel-and-toe steps.
5. Turn left.
6. Walk forward 2 heel-and-toe steps.

Try to imagine someone following these directions and leaving a path. What will this path look like?

Discuss the students' ideas. Select a student to follow the directions. Draw a representation of this student's path on the board and review the directions that created it.

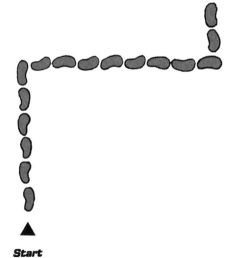

Start

Show the children how to turn on the computer and load Logo. Demonstrate simple Logo commands and explain how they make the turtle move. Show the students the following sequence of commands:

FD 60
RT 90
FD 80
LT 90
FD 20

How does the turtle's path compare with the path we walked? How are they alike? How are they different? Why? Encourage the children to use numbers and directions in their answers.

If you change a command, will the path drawn be the same or different? Why?

Change the FD 20 to FD 50, and ask the students to predict the path. Clear the screen and type this new sequence of commands to check their predictions. Repeat, changing LT 90 to RT 90.

Keep going. Have pairs of students complete the blackline master Turtle Time.

Encourage further interaction with the computer world of Logo by asking such questions as these:

How could you make the turtle walk other paths? Can you make it draw a square? A triangle? A rectangle? How many steps did you use?

Can you make the turtle draw a letter? Your initials?

Logo Commands:

FD = forward

RT = right

BK = back

LT = left

Commands for clearing the screen vary in Logo programs. Check your manual.

Domino Record Sheet

My domino	Total dots	One less	One more	My domino	Total dots	One less	One more
☐☐	___	___	___	☐☐	___	___	___
☐☐	___	___	___	☐☐	___	___	___
☐☐	___	___	___	☐☐	___	___	___
☐☐	___	___	___	☐☐	___	___	___
☐☐	___	___	___	☐☐	___	___	___

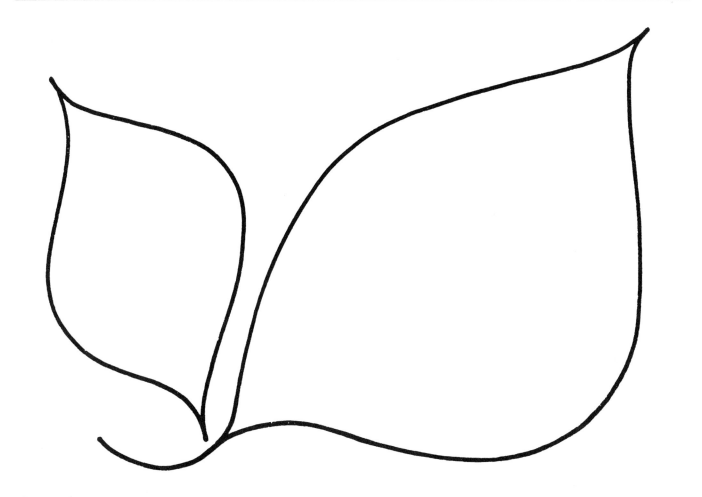

Turtle Time

In the Classroom: Child Steps

A. You are the turtle.

Walk the path.

1.   FD 5

2.   RT 90

3.   FD 5

4.   RT 90

5.   FD 5

6.   RT 90

7.   FD 5

B. Draw your path.

Start

In the Computer World: Turtle Steps

A. Clear the screen.

Type these commands:

    FD 50

    RT 90

    FD 80

    RT 90

    FD 50

    RT 90

B. Draw the path the turtle made.

C. Clear the screen. Place a small piece of masking tape somewhere on the screen. Give the command that will make the turtle hide under the masking tape on the screen. Could the turtle have gotten there with a shorter path?

Emphasizing exploratory experiences with numbers that capitalize on the natural insights of children enhances their sense of mathematical competency, enables them to build and extend number relationships, and helps them to develop a link between their world and the world of mathematics. (NCTM 1989a, p. 38)

If children have number sense, they understand the relationship of numbers to each other, are able to tell when an answer or a unit of measurement is reasonable, and can use numbers effectively in many situations. Number sense takes a long time to develop; even adults continue to grow in this ability. To establish an environment that nurtures the development of number sense in children, you will need to provide interesting questions to explore, suitable materials with which to investigate those questions, and a classroom climate that encourages the discussion and the display of the results of mathematical investigations.

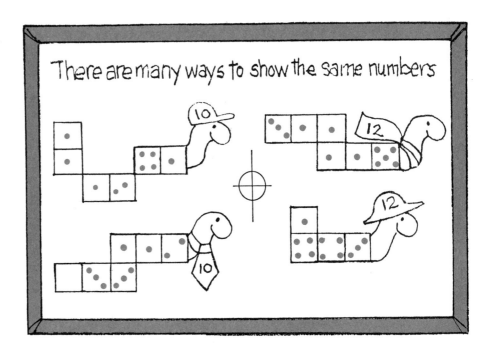

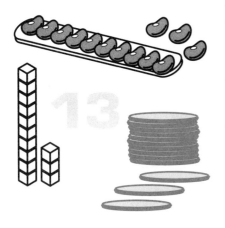

This bulletin board gives children a chance to show many ways to make the same sum. If they make large caterpillars, the children can use pressure sensitive dots to indicate the domino pips. The bulletin board itself is easily varied by changing the number on the caterpillar's tie or hat.

The first activity gives children a chance to practice basic addition and subtraction facts in a problem-solving context. In the next activity, children use models of odd and even numbers to explore simple sums. A third activity encourages children to use numbers and words to describe relationships on a calendar. The final activity presents students with a chance to use manipulative materials to solve problems involving two-digit addition and subtraction.

DOMINO CLOWNS

Get ready. The purpose of this activity is to have children find many different addends that give the same sum.

For each pair of students, you will need a set of dominoes, notebook paper, and a copy of the Domino Clowns blackline master (p. 24). If you do not have dominoes, you can easily make sets from 3" x 5" cards. Three dominoes, approximately 1 1/2" x 3", can be cut from each card.

Get going. Assign each pair of children a number from 15 to 30 and ask each child to find four dominoes that together have that number of dots. When they have done so, have the children put the dominoes on their clown as arms and legs. The children can verify their partner's sum and write on the notebook paper the number sentence that their own dominoes suggest.

Ask the children to choose another target number and repeat the activity several times. They will enjoy the challenge of discovering the largest possible sum that both partners can make using only one set of double 6 dominoes.

What would be the smallest sum that you could illustrate?

Suggest that the children use a calculator as they try to find dominoes that work.

Keep going. Later in the year you may want to use the Domino Clowns blackline master in an activity that focuses on renaming numbers and understanding place value. You will want to model the activity with the class before the children play alone. However, once the children understand how to play, this will be a good center activity.

Pairs of children have a Domino Clowns work mat and one set of double 6 dominoes. On each clown, the left side represents tens and the right side, ones. The object of the activity is to represent the greatest possible number. To play, the children turn the dominoes face down and draw them one at a time. Each domino must be placed as soon as it is drawn and may not be moved. As you model the activity, the children will discover that the number of ones on the right side as well as the number of tens on the left side may sometimes exceed 9. (For example, there may be 13 dots on the ones side and 8 dots on the tens side for a score of 93.) Since they need to name their numbers in standard form, some children may want to create addition problems.

Can you figure out your scores without writing down numbers to add?

Will you always have a renaming situation? [No, a clown may have 7 dots on the ones side and 5 dots on the tens side for a score of 57.]

ODDS AND EVENS

Get ready. The purpose of this activity is to introduce children to the patterns resulting from the addition of odd and even numbers.

Each pair of students will need twenty-one counters, two sheets of graph paper with large squares, scissors, and a single die.

Get going. Begin by asking the students if they could use their counters to model some numbers that are even and some that are odd. Have the students explain so that all children will be able to model examples. Ask them to use their counters to model all the numbers on their die and to group the models into odd numbers and even numbers. Each student should record the models on graph paper and cut out the six models.

Recording sheets may be used in a variety of ways. You can create four answer sheets from one blackline master. Ask questions such as these: How much money is in each cup? How much does each object weigh? How long is each ribbon?

Name _____	Name _____
A. _____	A. _____
B. _____	B. _____
C. _____	C. _____
D. _____	D. _____
E. _____	E. _____
F. _____	F. _____
Name _____	Name _____
A. _____	A. _____
B. _____	B. _____
C. _____	C. _____
D. _____	D. _____
E. _____	E. _____
F. _____	F. _____

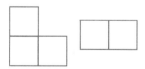

"I know that 2 is an even number because there are no blocks without a partner, but 3 is odd because one block sticks out by itself," said Katie.

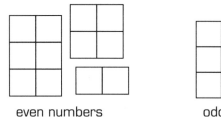
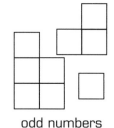

even numbers   odd numbers

Addend	Addend	Sum
3 odd	5 odd	8 even
3 odd	4 even	7 odd
2 even	7 odd	9 odd
6 even	2 even	8 even

Have the children take turns rolling the die and identifying the number rolled as odd or even. Tell the partners to add their numbers by putting their paper models together and to state if the sum is odd or even. Encourage them to roll their die several times and to model each addend and the sum of the addends, each time telling each other about the sum.

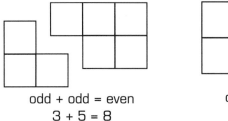
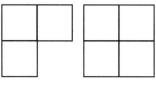

odd + odd = even   odd + even = odd
3 + 5 = 8   3 + 4 = 7

Keep going. When you are certain your students understand the task, have each pair make a table like that shown at the right as they roll their die and model the sums. After they have entered several lines in the table, ask them if they see any patterns and to describe what they notice. Suggest that they test their conjectures with other numbers. Encourage the children to explain in their own words their findings that the sum of two even numbers is even, that the sum of two odd numbers is even, and that the sum of an even number and an odd number is odd.

HOW BIG IS IT?

Get ready. The purpose of this activity is to help children discover that as the size of a measuring unit varies, the number of units needed to measure also varies. Through practice, we want them to discover that as the size of a measuring unit increases, the number of units needed to measure a given object decreases; as the size of the measuring unit decreases, the number of units needed to measure the same object increases.

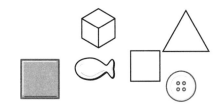

What I used	Guess	Test

Give each pair of students sheets of plain paper and ask them to draw around each other's foot. Then provide regular units of several kinds for students to use in covering one footprint. You might use paper squares, interlocking cubes, pattern blocks, or small crackers.

Have them make a chart with the columns labeled WHAT I USED, GUESS, and TEST.

Get going. Have each pair of students choose and record a unit, guess how many of that unit will be needed to cover each footprint, and record the guess. Now have the students cover each footprint with the unit, count how many units were needed, and record the number next to their guess. When the children have completed the task with several different units, ask questions such as these:

What unit gave you the smallest number? The largest? Why do you think that was so?

Keep going. Prepare a blackline master on which an irregular shape, such as that of a cartoon character or an apple, is drawn. Have the students use a familiar unit to measure the selected shape. You might also wish to give the students other units and ask them to use the data they collected to predict how many of the new units will be needed to cover the shape.

After the children have explored with several different units, have them graph the number of each unit used. They could trace the units used on the horizontal axis and color in boxes that represent the number of that type of unit that was used.

CALENDAR ACTIVITIES

Get ready. The purpose of this activity is to have children continue to develop mathematical vocabulary related to time and an understanding of time passage. In addition to your daily references to the date, you may want to spend some time investigating the calendar for the month.

A large classroom calendar is needed for daily explorations; for some activities, the students will need a calendar for the month on which they may write.

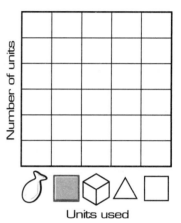

Units used

Get going. Routinely ask questions like these:

What is today's date? What was yesterday's date? What date will tomorrow be? In two days, what will be the date?

How many days are there in this month? What day of the week is today? How many more days until Sunday? Last week, on what date was Sunday? What date will one week from today be? Two weeks from next Saturday will be what date?

Ask the children to compare the number of school days with the total number of days in the month.

Which number will be greater?

What number should be added to today's date to find the date in exactly one week?

What two numbers could be added to get today's date?

Why is it not possible to have six Saturdays in a month?

Have the children draw a big X on the calendar, as illustrated, to connect the days in two weeks.

MAY						
		1	2	3	4	5
6	7	8	9	10	11	12
13	14	15	16	17	18	19
20	21	22	23	24	25	26
27	28	29	30	31		

Use your calculator to add the two numbers joined by each line. What do you notice?

Try this again with other pairs of days. Why do you think you are getting similar results?

If you make your X bigger and add three numbers in a row, what do you think will happen?

Keep going. Encourage the children to create similar problems and solve each other's questions. Suggest that they look for patterns on the calendar as they create new puzzles and describe orally or in writing the patterns they find.

BEANSTICK ADDITION

Get ready. The purpose of this activity is to have children explore the effectiveness and usefulness of addition and subtraction algorithms.

Give each child a copy of the Addition work mat (p. 25), ten beansticks, and a handful of loose beans. If you prefer, interlocking cubes can be used for this activity.

To make beansticks, have the students glue ten beans on each stick with white glue. Let the sticks dry. Durability is increased when a thin ribbon of glue is applied along the top of the beans and allowed to run down onto the sticks and dry.

Get going. If the manipulative is to be useful, it must have meaning for the students. They must make connections between the symbols and the materials. Therefore, before the students use their beansticks to add or subtract, they need to use them to model numbers. Each beanstick represents a ten and each loose bean, a one. Have them model counting by tens:

Show 30; show 80; show 40.

Have the students then model the "in between" numbers:

Show 17; show 46; show 35.

Most students will show 35 as 3 tens and 5 ones.

Could 35 also be 2 tens and 15 ones?

Build a number on the overhead projector with beansticks and have the students tell what you are modeling.

If I add another beanstick, what will the number be?

What if I build 58 and add 6 more loose beans? Could I do any trading?

When you are confident that the manipulatives are meaningful to the students, ask two students to each name a two-digit number less than 50 (for example, 38 and 45). Then ask the class to make up a story in which these two numbers would need to be added. Record the problem on the overhead projector or at the chalkboard for all to see. Encourage the students to decide what the total will be and record all the answers.

Ask the students if their beansticks would be helpful in finding an answer to the problem. Call on several students to share their thinking with the class. Repeat the activity several times. No attempt should be made to restrict the addends to those that will not require renaming.

Keep going. The following activity, which uses the Addition work mat, is more structured and closely models the algorithm for addition.

Consider setting up a beanstick factory in one corner of your classroom. Students could learn about assembly lines, quality control, and working in shifts. Cover the work area with wax paper, since white glue will pop off the wax paper easily when the glue is dry. The power of this activity is in the process of the students' creating a place value manipulative.

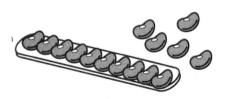

By emphasizing underlying concepts, using physical materials to model procedures, linking the manipulation of materials to the steps of the procedures, and developing thinking patterns, teachers can help children master basic facts and algorithms and understand their usefulness and relevance to daily situations. (NCTM 1989a, p. 44)

Have the students put three beansticks in the upper left box and six beans in the upper right box. Tell the students to write the number 36 in the recording box at the bottom of the page. Then have them put four beansticks and five beans in the lower set of boxes and record those numbers. Ask the students how they could use the beans and beansticks to find each sum.

Are there more than 10 loose beans? What could we do? How could we record what we are doing?

You may wish to have a child read the exercise aloud, *36 + 45 = 81,* while another records the number sentence on the overhead projector or at the chalkboard. Throughout the exercise, reinforce the concepts that the students are adding 36 and 45 and that these are not two separate problems in which they add 6 and 5 and then 3 and 4—as if the numbers all represented ones.

Suggest to the students that they extend the procedure to adding three-digit numbers. If you do this, have the students first make beanstick rafts by attaching craft sticks crosswise to the backs of ten beansticks, as illustrated.

Beanstick subtraction can be developed in an analogous way. The recording sheet would look like the sample below. Ask the children to make up a story using subtraction. Have them put beansticks and beans on the work mat to model the story and write the number in the top section of a recording box. On the basis of their story, they should decide how many to take away and write that number in the bottom section of the recording box. Note that the number to be subtracted is *not* being modeled because it is contained within the original set. Encourage the students to explain in different ways how they would subtract.

What should we do with our beansticks to show what is happening in our story? How could we record this?

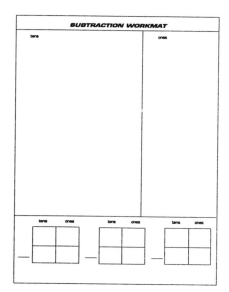

As children work with their beansticks and beans, encourage them to record each completed step.

It is important for children to learn the sequence of steps—and the reasons for them—in the pencil-and-paper algorithms used widely in our culture. (NCTM 1989a, p. 47)

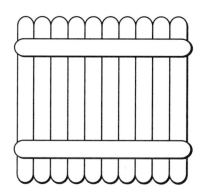

(W)hen children's understanding is ... closely tied to the use of physical materials, assessment tasks that allow them to use such materials are better indicators of learning. (NCTM 1989a, p. 96)

Domino Clowns

ADDITION WORK MAT

tens

ones

tens

ones

	tens	ones		tens	ones		tens	ones
$+$			$+$			$+$		

CHAPTER 4
THIRD GRADE

Number sense develops over many years, and there may be a wide disparity in this area among any class of third-grade students. The understanding they possess will be fostered if they model numbers in many ways and use numbers to describe real-world situations.

Research over the past few decades has demonstrated that children learn best when they are actively investigating, discussing, and reporting questions of interest. All the activities in this section encourage active learning and focus on estimation and multiplication.

STREETS AND AVENUES

Get ready. The purpose of this activity is to have children explore multiplication as an array model. Each group of students needs toothpicks, glue, and paper and a pencil for recording.

Get going. Have the children use toothpicks and glue to build maps showing the streets and the avenues of a small town (where streets intersect avenues at right angles) and use a marker to indicate where stoplights are needed.

How many crossing points for stoplights can you make with two (three, four, five,...) toothpicks? Have the students use toothpicks to make maps to show the possible arrangements.

Can you arrange four toothpicks so that there would be no stoplights? [Yes] *One stoplight?* [No]

What is the largest number of stoplights you can have? [4]

Maps with four toothpicks

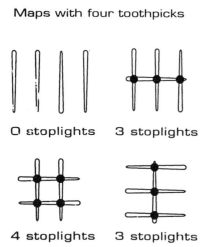

0 stoplights   3 stoplights

4 stoplights   3 stoplights

Help the students organize their findings in a table by recording the number of streets, avenues, and stoplights needed with four toothpicks.

Keep going. This activity provides the students an opportunity to use manipulative materials to investigate products and factors in rectangular arrays. They can also use a pictorial model by drawing line segments and counting points of intersection. Suggest that different groups explore with different numbers of toothpicks. Have them record the maps and organize the data numerically in a table. Relate to multiplication facts.

Number of toothpicks	Number of streets	Number of avenues	Number of stoplights
4	4	0	0
4	3	1	3
4	2	2	4
4	1	3	3
4	0	4	0

Multiplication facts
$4 \times 0 = 0$
$3 \times 1 = 3$
$2 \times 2 = 4$
$1 \times 3 = 3$
$0 \times 4 = 0$

BUNCHES OF BEANS

Get ready. The purpose of this activity is to engage students in a series of estimation tasks to develop estimation strategies and a better sense of the reasonableness of results.

Set aside a space in your classroom to display the question of the week and the student responses. In the same area, place a transparent jar filled with dry beans. In subsequent weeks you can vary this activity by using several identical transparent jars or various kinds of dry beans, marbles, or other objects of different sizes.

Get going. Each Monday, post a question for the week, such as, How many lima beans are in the jar?

Encourage the students to estimate the number and show how they arrived at the estimate. At the end of the week, discuss the set of

Times of free exploration offer many opportunities to informally evaluate individual students' understanding of mathematical ideas. While children are engaged with the materials, move around the classroom to assess students' use of various counting strategies and estimation skills.

answers received. Graph them with sticky squares. Ask questions such as the following:

Were some estimates near each other? What was the smallest estimate? The largest?

Was there a number most estimates were near?

Have the children open the jar and count the beans. Were most of the estimates close to the correct answer?

Discuss the students' strategies for estimation. The students may begin estimating by mentally grouping the objects into tens and hundreds. This should be encouraged, especially since it reinforces place-value concepts.

Keep going. Provide several identical jars, each with beans of a different size. Keep the jars of beans from previous weeks' investigations in the question area along with a file of the corresponding data. These will encourage students to use their earlier estimates and counts as they make their new predictions. Vary the size of the containers and the contents throughout the year. Consider making a small group of students responsible for counting the objects and putting them in the containers. They should record the number, but keep it a secret until everyone has made all the estimates.

POPCORN PREDICTIONS

This lesson includes many science concepts. Connections between mathematical topics and language arts are also featured in this activity.

Get ready. The purpose of this activity is to help students apply their estimation skills and develop a better sense of the relative magnitude of numbers.

Make a transparency of the Popcorn Grid blackline master (p. 32) and cut it in half. Divide the class into groups and give each group a copy of Popcorn Predictions (p. 33), a copy of the 2 x 5 grid from the Popcorn Grids master, and a one-half cup of popcorn kernels in a paper cup. Have available scales, various containers for the popped corn (jars, paper bags in at least two sizes, and cans), scoops, bowls, a hot-air popper, and cookie sheets or large pieces of clean paper to catch the container overflow. Since they will be eating the popcorn later, make sure that the children wash their hands.

Get going. Give each group of children a set of the materials. Tell them to guess how many kernels there are in their group's container.

Discuss how they might estimate in a systematic way without actually counting the kernels. One way is to count out ten or twenty kernels, and then estimate the number in the cup. Another strategy is to use a grid to help estimate. On the overhead projector, show the transparency picturing popcorn kernels. Then place the 2 x 5 grid on top of it. Ask the students if determining how many kernels are in one rectangle will help them in estimating the total number. Discuss the strategies they invent. Repeat the estimation by placing popcorn kernels randomly on the overhead projector and using the 2 x 5 grid. Discuss whether the strategies are always applicable. What would happen if the popcorn were not evenly spaced?

Have the students use their grid paper to make an estimate of the number of kernels their group has by pouring the kernels onto the grid paper and spreading them out to cover the paper. Students within each group should agree on an estimate and record it on their copies of Popcorn Predictions.

Have the groups share their estimates and demonstrate and discuss how they arrived at them.

Ask the students if they think that the weight of the kernels before and after popping will be the same. Have them estimate the size of the container needed to hold the popped kernels from one-half cup of popcorn, the time it will take to pop the kernels, and the number of kernels that will not pop. Have them record their estimates on their worksheet. Do the experiment and discuss their findings.

Why does the weight change? [The popped corn weighs less because it loses moisture when the steam escapes.]

Have the students make lists of adjectives to describe popped and unpopped corn.

Why does popcorn pop? [Corn seeds contain moisture that turns to steam when heated. The expanding steam cracks the shell.]

Keep going. You may wish to extend this activity in several ways:

Have the students compare the popping time and the popping success rate of several brands of popcorn and graph the results.

Do all brands of popcorn pop the same? If you started with one-fourth cup of kernels, how many cups of popcorn would you get for each brand? How many kernels remain unpopped from each batch? How do the

◆   ◆   ◆   ◆   ◆   ◆   ◆   ◆   ◆

In their mathematics journals, ask students to write about the popcorn lesson, describing the different activities within the lesson. Ask them to reflect on how they might improve their estimation skills.

results of your experiment compare with the results of the June 1989 Consumer's Report *article on popcorn and popcorn poppers?*

Encourage the students to determine their preferences for corn popped in an oil popper, a microwave oven, or a hot-air popper. They might graph the results of the survey or write a report for the school newspaper or display their findings on the wall outside the classroom.

Challenge the students to find a strategy for determining the weight of a single kernel of corn.

NEWSPAPER SCAVENGER HUNT

Get ready. The purpose of this activity is to have students develop an awareness of the many ways they use numbers in their daily lives.

Materials needed include a newspaper, glue, crayons, and a copy of Newspaper Scavenger Hunt (p. 34) for each group of children.

When mathematical ideas are also connected to everyday experiences, both in and out of school, children become aware of the usefulness of mathematics.
(NCTM 1989a, p. 32)

Building students' ability to think independently helps them sense that they are controlling and creating mathematics.

Get going. Give each group a set of materials. Remind them to work together to complete the task. As they find each item, they should cut it out and glue it next to its description on the Newspaper Scavenger Hunt recording sheet.

Keep going. After all the teams have found all the items, you may wish to extend the activity. Some suggestions follow:

Have the students classify the numbers they found into two or more groups by circling the numbers with different colored crayons. When they have done so, ask them to explain the basis of their sorting.

Have the students write a paragraph on how numbers are used in their own lives.

Have each team develop another scavenger hunt using newspapers, textbooks, or library materials. Students should be instructed not to cut up the books, but to record the book title and the page where the number was found. Have them exchange the new worksheets and repeat the activity with the student-generated "hunts." Students could also develop scavenger hunts for numbers in history, literature, science, and other areas.

USING A DATA BANK

Get ready. The purpose of this activity is to have students generate and solve word problems using realistic data.

Give each group of two students a copy of the Data Bank (p.35).

Get going. With the whole class, discuss the data base and brainstorm about problems that could be generated from that data base.

Challenge the students to create problems that contain two or more operations. When the children have written the problems, have them trade their sheets with their partners, estimate the answers, and use calculators to solve the problems. You may wish to have the students write and solve their problems on the overhead projector or at the chalkboard. Have the students edit their problems and write them on individual file cards for sharing with other classes or for placing in a mathematics center.

Follow-up discussions are perhaps the most valuable part of this type of activity. They should help students clarify their ideas and write more intelligibly. Ask the students to answer the questions, "What makes a good problem?" and "Why are some problems more interesting than others?" Encourage the children to defend their answers.

Make connections to science by relating the data bank to the study of energy and calories.

Keep going. There are many ways to extend this activity.

Encourage the students to collect similar data from cereal boxes or cookbooks at home and to construct another data bank.

Have them plan a meal and estimate how many calories it contains. How many calories do they need in a day?

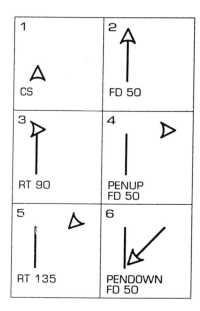

Provide restaurant menus and pose problems with several answers, such as "If you receive $2.15 in change, what did you buy and how much money did you give the waiter?" Emphasize students' explanations and reasoning.

POPCORN GRID

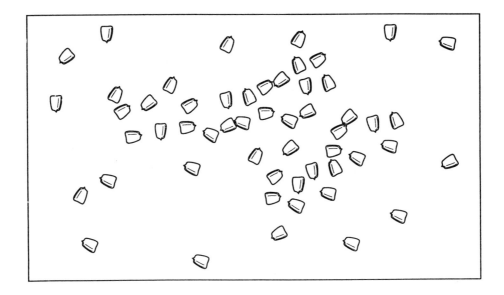

POPCORN PREDICTIONS

I. MEASURE OUT ONE-HALF CUP OF POPCORN KERNELS.

    A. How many kernels do you think there are? _____

       Work as a group to make an estimate without counting all pieces. _____

       How did you make your estimate?_____

       _____

    B. Make another estimate using the grid. _____

       Tell how you made this estimate. _____

       _____

    C. Count. Record the number. _____

       How close to the actual number were the two estimates? _____

       Was using a grid a helpful strategy? Why or why not? _____

       _____

II. CHOOSE A CONTAINER THAT YOU THINK WILL HOLD ALL THE POPPED KERNELS.

    A. Answer all the questions in part A before going on to part B.

       How much do the unpopped kernels weigh? _____

       How much do you think the popped kernels will weigh? _____

       How many minutes will the corn take to pop? _____

       How many kernels do you think will be unpopped? _____

    B. Pop the corn. How long did it take to pop the corn? _____

       Pour your popped corn into the container you chose.

       Was the container too big? Too little? Just right? _____

       How many kernels were unpopped? _____

       How much do the popped kernels weigh? _____

       Write two things you learned by doing these experiments.

       _____

       _____

       _____

NEWSPAPER SCAVENGER HUNT

Names of your team members: _____   _____

_____   _____

In a newspaper, find the following items, cut them out, and paste your examples next to the description.

1. The price of something to eat

2. A street address

3. A number that gives a size

4. A phone number

5. The date the paper was published

6. A number in a recipe

7. A number that names a distance

8. A number that names a temperature

9. A number written in words

10. The score of a game

DATA BANK

FOOD	AMOUNT	CALORIES
bran flakes	2/3 cup	90
corn flakes	1 cup	110
toasted oat cereal	2/3 cup	110
puffed wheat	1 cup	60
raisin bran	2/3 cup	120
whole milk	8 oz.	160
2 percent milk	8 oz.	145
skim milk	8 oz.	90
banana	1	100
peach	1	35
sugar	1 tablespoon	40

Write two problems using the data in the data bank.

Problem 1: _____

_____

_____

Problem 2: _____

_____

_____

CHAPTER 5
FOURTH GRADE

As in the earlier grades, the assessment of students' ability to understand mathematical terms and concepts is best achieved through a natural extension of instructional activities. Such questions as "Why?" "What if?" and "How would you convince someone?" should be asked routinely to help students explain or justify their answers or conjectures. (NCTM 1989a, p. 216)

In the fourth grade, students typically begin a more intensive study of fractions and decimals. Extending their understanding of whole numbers becomes a major focus of the mathematics program. This section presents a sample of whole and rational number problem-solving activities and illustrates appropriate teaching strategies. For example, you might engage students in short, warm-up activities every day to bring number sense to the fore. In all lessons that involve numbers—in and beyond mathematics—encourage children to use estimation and mental arithmetic whenever feasible. When a calculator is the most appropriate tool, encourage and support its use.

THE QUILT FACTORY

Get ready. The purpose of this activity is to have children apply their knowledge of fractions at concrete and pictorial levels in a creative situation.

Give each student scissors and crayons and several square sheets of plain paper (for part 1) or several sheets of 1" grid paper (for part 2).

Get going.

Part 1. Describing designs

Ask the students to fold a square to make either two or three equal parts. Have them fold the square again once or twice as suggested by the diagram, which shows an example of three folds. Encourage the children to invent alternative ways of folding.

Students' ability to understand the written and oral communication of others is an important component of instruction and assessment. (NCTM 1989a, p. 214)

 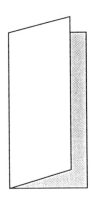 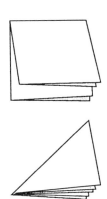

Ask the students to make a design by coloring the parts of the folded square. Have them describe their completed work. Encourage numerical descriptions.

How many equal parts did you divide your squares into? What would we call one of these parts? How would you describe your designs by color?

The art teacher may wish to work with you in presenting this activity.

Have the students mount their designs and write about how they created them. Use the designs and reports for a bulletin board display.

Repeat the activity. Once the students have finished coloring, have them describe the design to their partners, who then attempt to duplicate it without seeing the model. Tell the students to use fractional language whenever possible to describe the parts.

Part 2. Replicating quilt patterns

Enlarge one of the quilt designs illustrated below. Suggest that the children copy it onto dot paper, devise a coloring pattern, and decide what part of the design will be a given color. Have them color the quilt pattern and check the fractional amount colored. When the students are ready, have them discuss their artwork and tell how they arrived at each fractional estimate.

Connections between mathematics and other subjects, such as social studies, enrich both subjects and help students value mathematics.

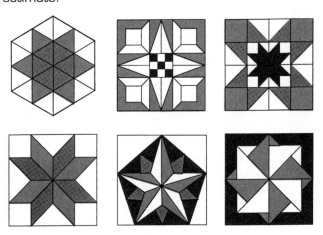

You may extend this activity by asking questions such as the following:

Is your design symmetric? How do you know?

How could we group the designs?

If your design were a dart board, what color would you be most likely to hit if you threw one dart? Would a dart be more likely to hit a purple section or a white one? Why?

Keep going. Have each student decide which of the student-designed squares has the largest fraction of a given color. To check, lay a transparent grid over the square. You can make such a grid by running coordinate paper through a transparency maker. This grid will also be handy for demonstrating a particular coloring pattern on the overhead projector.

Ask students to create a design that conforms to given specifications, such as ¼ blue, ¼ blue and green stripe, ½ green. When they finish, ask them to defend their coloring decisions. Encourage the students to use resource materials to discover traditional quilt designs and to discuss why people made quilts from small pieces of material. [Cloth and woven blankets were very expensive. Quilted bed coverings were warm and made good use of the pieces left over from making clothing or snipped from clothing too worn to wear.]

If students create a design that is 8/16 purple and replicate it three more times, ask what part of the entire 4-block design is purple. Notice that many students count squares whereas some recognize the relationship between the similar designs.

Use the quilt pieces to make a class bulletin board. Construct large group quilts—possibly made from all the designs that fit the same "given specifications"—and hang them on display. Stories describing what was done, giving historical contexts and so on, might accompany the quilts.

If you choose to make large quilts, you might have students replicate their designs so that they have four congruent designs. Assemble these four pieces into a large square and glue these large squares onto background paper to make several quilts for each class.

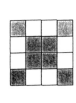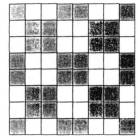

As a variation, encourage the students to make a quilt of squares that tell about themselves, such as their hobbies, favorite colors and activities, friends, and so on. Have them describe their personal square.

SPROUTING SEEDS

Get ready. The purpose of this activity is to have students apply fraction concepts in a science setting.

For each team of four students you will need paper towels, four transparent plastic cups, masking tape, sixty seeds (in an envelope) from a bag of birdseed or alfafa, plastic wrap, and, if possible, a hand lens.

Extend the science ideas in this lesson to include other factors that affect seed growth.

Get going. Discuss germination rates (the fractional part of a group of seeds that is expected to sprout). Furnish each team with the supplies listed above and have them divide the seeds in the envelope so each student in the group has the same number. When the whole team is satisfied that they have completed the task, have each member use the masking tape to label a cup with his or her name. Give the following instructions:

Counting and predicting lead naturally to topics such as probability and statistics.

Cover the bottom of each cup with a wet paper towel, then place your seeds on the towel. Make a lid from plastic wrap, cover the cup, and put it where it can be observed but remain undisturbed for several days. Make sure that the seeds are kept moist.

When they see the first growth, have the students write their estimates of the fractional part of the seeds they expect to sprout. Show the children that if they expect 10 of their 15 seeds to sprout, they can write $^{10}/_{15}$. Remind the students that they are estimating the fractional part that sprouts, not the time it takes to sprout. After the seeds have sprouted, have the students determine the germination rates for their seeds, express the rates as fractions, and compare their estimates to the actual germination rate.

Questions such as "What fractional part of your seeds sprouted?" can be used to guide class discussion. Lay the foundation for the concept of ratio by asking such questions as "Amy had 15 seeds and 10 sprouted. What fractional part of the seeds sprouted and what part did not sprout? If she had 30 seeds how many would she expect to sprout?"

Keep going. A rich variety of activities can grow out of these beginnings. Choose from the following challenges:

♦ Compare the germination rate for various kinds of seeds in a seed mixture.

♦ Find the germination rate across the whole classroom for the different types of seeds. Discuss what students would predict if they were to repeat the experiment (do so if there is time).

♦ Examine commercial seed packets or catalogs to discover the projected germination rates of various seeds. Share these data by means of a graph. If rates are given in percentages, explain that these are sprouting rates for every one hundred seeds.

♦ Sprout such seeds as mung bean, radish, alfalfa, and cabbage (available from health food stores). Conduct a tasting party with the sprouts when they are about five to seven centimeters long.

♦ Measure and graph the growing rates of different seeds under various conditions (sunny window, warm closet, salted water).

HISTORICAL VOYAGES

Get ready. The purpose of this activity is to have children make estimations on the basis of independent readings in science and history.

Get going. Note that people as well as plants need water. Discuss the problem of people at sea who cannot drink the salt water. Pose the following problem:

How much water might Columbus have carried for his trip across the Atlantic? What do you need to know to make an estimate? Where could you start to find this information? Who could help you besides your teacher?

Have the students check reference books for information on the number of people, the length of the trip, the amount of water people need each day, and so on, to make reasoned estimates of the amount of water needed. Discuss how much space would be needed to store the water for the trip.

Keep going. Solve similar problems involving Marco Polo, Matthew Henson, Charles Lindberg, Amelia Earhart, astronauts going to the

School mathematics must endow all students with a realization that doing mathematics is a common human activity. Having numerous and varied experiences allows students to trust their own mathematical thinking. (NCTM 1989a, p. 6)

This activity makes connections to history, science, geography, and other areas of mathematics.

Measurement, number sense, and problem solving come together in tasks such as this: Suppose we had to store a week's supply of water in our classroom. Each student needs at least five 8-ounce glasses of water each day. How much water would we need and how would we store it?

Roald Amundsen

Roald Amundsen from Norway discoved the South Pole in 1906. He had a crew of _____ people and _____ dogs. They planned to be gone for _____ months. They needed _____ kilograms food and _____ liters of water.

moon, and so on. Have each child chose his or her favorite explorer and prepare similar questions for other students to answer.

Understanding multiple representations for numbers is a crucial precursor to solving many of the problems students encounter. (NCTM 1989a, p. 87)

Depending on the size of the numbers, you may wish to provide calculators for this activity.

Making conjectures, gathering evidence, and building an argument to support such notions are fundamental to doing mathematics. In fact, a demonstration of good reasoning should be rewarded even more than students' ability to find correct answers. (NCTM 1989a, p. 6)

MINI-MATH MOMENTS—WAYS TO TURN WAITING TIME INTO LEARNING TIME

The Answer Is...

Get ready. The purpose of this activity is to give children mental arithmetic opportunities.

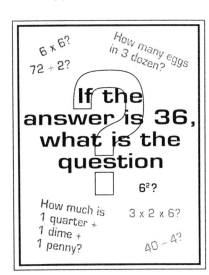

Get going. Announce a number and ask each student in turn to state a question for which that number is the answer. Give the students several examples to encourage nonroutine thinking. ("The answer is 36." Possible questions: "What is 3×12?"; "What is $3 \times 2 \times 6$?"; "How much money is one quarter, one dime, and one penny?"; "What is six more than the number of days in November?"; "What is the number of inches in three feet?") Make large posters for each answer and the questions it generated.

Encourage the students to record a list of some answers and questions on adding-machine paper. Display the list on parents' night and have visitors add to it.

Keep going. Change the focus from giving many descriptions of a known number to discovering an unknown number, "the answer," through a series of progressive clues. For example, if "the answer" is 7, you might give the class these clues:

> I am less than 10.
> I am an odd number.
> I am more than 6.
> I am a prime number.

Show the clues one at a time and encourage the students to give possible answers after each clue is uncovered.

After you model several of these "What number am I?" puzzles, have the students write their own for others to solve. You may wish to give them guidelines, such as the riddles must have at least four clues but no more than seven clues or the riddles should have two possible answers.

Make It More, Make It Less

Get ready. The purpose of this activity is to have students use their knowledge of number and place value in mental arithmetic.

Each pair of students will need a number cube labeled 1 through 6.

Get going. The purpose of the game is to reach either 0 or 100 by deciding what operation to use on each successive randomly generated number. Pair the students and have each student begin by writing down 50. To play, the first student rolls the number cube, decides whether to add, subtract, multiply, or divide the two numbers (the number rolled and the number written), performs the operation, and records the result on his or her paper. Then it is the second student's turn. Play continues until one partner reaches either 100 or 0.

Beginning number	Number rolled	Operation	Ending number
50	6	–	44
44	4	÷	11
11	5	–	6
6	2	?	?

What operation might this student choose in round 4?

Keep going. An option is to use two or more number cubes and allow a combination of operations. You can also use number cubes marked 10 through 60, a starting point of 500, and a goal of 1000 or 0.

For a whole-class activity, roll a number cube ten times. For each roll, each student must decide to multiply the number rolled by 1, 10, or 100 and then sum the ten products. The student whose sum is closest to 1000 is the winner.

Dateline

Get ready. The purposes of this activity are to have students discover different ways to express a given number and to reinforce the order of operations.

Get going. Using this format, write the date 1/8/91. Have the students use any operations desired and those four digits arranged in any order to arrive at a given target number, such as 1. (Example: 1 + 9 – 8 – 1 = 1) Have the students write their solutions on the overhead projector or on the chalkboard.

My birthday is 2/25/82.
My favorite numbers are 7 and 12.
$\frac{2}{2} + 5 + 8 - 2 = 12$
$22 - 5 - 8 - 2 = 7$

Ryan

◆　　◆　　◆　　◆　　◆　　◆　　◆　　◆

Keep going. Develop a similar activity by using many other sets of digits, such as four 4s, five 5s, someone's birth date, or the digits of the year.

Challenge the students to use the digits 1, 2, 3, 4, 5, 6, 7, 8, and 9, in that order, with any operation sign to reach 100. For example, 123 – 4 – 5 – 6 – 7 + 8 – 9 = 100.

Can you find another solution? Do you think there are more?

Challenge another class to find more solutions. Post the latest solution along with the student's picture on your door.

Fill It Up

Get ready. The purpose of this activity is to have students practice written computation that emphasizes knowledge of place value and strategic thinking.

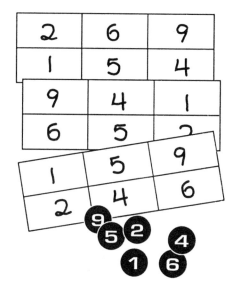

You need slips of paper or disks numbered 0 through 9 and a bag from which to draw them.

Get going. Have the students draw a 2 × 3 array on their paper.

Tell them that you will draw a disk from the bag and call out the number. As they hear the number, they must write it in one of the six rectangles. Once they write the number they cannot move it. You will draw a disk in this way six times, replacing the disk in the bag after each selection.

When six numbers have been called and all the children have added their numbers, call on one child to give his or her sum.

Did anyone get a higher sum?

Have a student explain how he or she got it.

Is there a still higher sum? Is there another way to get that sum?

What is the lowest sum you could get with these six numbers? In how many ways can you get that sum?

If we use a 3 × 2 array instead of the 2 × 3 array, will you change your strategy? How? Which array will yield larger sums? Why?

Keep going. You may vary this activity as follows:

◆ Do not replace the disks after selecting each one. Ask the students how that will change their strategy.

◆ Draw seven disks; players may erase and replace exactly one number.

◆ Use a 3 × 2 array or a 2 × 4 array.

◆ Have the children subtract the numbers. The goal is to get the largest difference.

◆ Have the children subtract the numbers. The goal is to get the difference closest to zero.

◆ Have the students draw two boxes over one box to create a format for multiplication.

◆ Where should I put the largest number to get the largest product?

◆ Challenge them to extend their results to other numbers of digits. You may wish to allow the students to use calculators.

◆ Use a format for division with a one-digit divisor and a four-digit dividend.

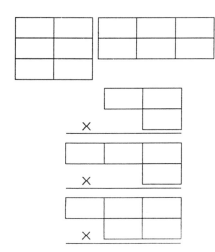

Lead the students in discussing the different strategies they used for the different operations. Use calculators to explore the same activity with decimals. See if the strategies are different using decimals.

CHAPTER 6
FIFTH GRADE

Children with number sense use numbers flexibly and choose the most appropriate representation of a number for a given circumstance. When solving problems, they are able to select from various strategies and tools—they know when to estimate, when to use paper and pencil, and when to use a calculator. They predict with some accuracy the result of an operation and describe the relationships between various forms of numbers. Both on tests and in real-world situations, fifth graders model and use numbers in many ways to assess the results of their mathematical reasoning.

Active fifth graders enjoy working together to investigate puzzling events and to solve mysteries. Activities presented here capitalize on students' curiosity by motivating them to explore mathematical questions and to make and verify predictions.

As they learn new ideas or solve new problems, students enrich their own thought processes and skills by drawing on previously developed ideas; this ability to integrate ideas and concepts fosters students' confidence in their own thinking as well as in their skills of communication. (NCTM 1989a, p. 85)

To provide students with a lasting sense of number and number relationships, learning should be grounded in experience related to aspects of everyday life or to the use of concrete materials designed to reflect underlying mathematical ideas. (NCTM 1989a, p. 87)

FIND THE MISSING LINK

Get ready. The purpose of this activity is to have students practice estimating and computing with decimals. Being able to place the correct number in the link requires facility with both estimation and computation. Determining the missing link provides a bridge from arithmetic to algebra. Calculator use is an integral part of this activity.

On an overhead transparency, draw chains such as the one shown. Write decimal numbers in the first four links.

$$19.7 \; (+) \; 13.4 \; (-) \; 12.5 \; (+) \; 8.2 \; (=)$$

Get going. For each problem, ask the students to look at the chain, estimate the answer, and explain how they arrived at the estimate. For the problem above, a student said that she estimated by rounding to 20 + 10 - 10 + 8, or 28. Another student explained that the difference between 13.4 and 12.5 is about 1; his estimate was 20 + 1 + 8, or 29. Pose questions to the class to encourage a variety of estimation strategies and to reinforce computational skills.

Opportunities to explain, conjecture, and defend one's ideas orally and in writing can stimulate deeper understandings of concepts and principles. (NCTM 1989a, p. 78)

When students find the numeric value of a missing link, they are, in fact, solving an algebraic equation where the empty link takes the place of the variable, x.

 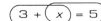

Student responses:

Merrie: "I subtracted 3 from 6 and then added 5. I got 8, so I had to subtract 2 to get 6 on the right-hand side."

Ralph: "I added 6 and 5 and got 11. I subtracted 3 and got 8, which was 2 more than 6. So I put 2 in the empty link."

Some types of link problems:

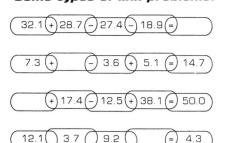

Will the answer be more that 20? More than 30? How do you know?

Will the order in which you do the calculations make a difference?

Suppose we add 10 to each number in the problem. How would that affect the result?

Allow ample time for class discussion. Calculators can be used throughout the activity to determine good estimates and to compute answers. Do several examples of the same type before proceeding to more challenging problems.

Display another chain, such as the one below. Pose questions and accept suggestions from the class as you work together to estimate and solve the problem.

Is this one harder to solve? Why?

Explore other links with the class. Encourage further class discussion.

Is more than one answer possible?

What is the smallest number that you think can be put in the first link?

What is the largest number that you feel can be put in the next open link?

Challenge the class with problems with missing operations, such as the one below.

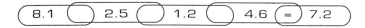

If addition, subtraction, and multiplication were used to form the chain above, what other answers are possible?

Discuss any variations that may be suggested and include the use of whole numbers and fractions in the missing link problems.

Keep going. Put the students in small groups and have them generate their own missing link problems. Suggest that each student group keep answer keys for their problems. Ask them to exchange their problems with other groups.

SKATING OFF THE SNACK

Get ready. The purpose of this activity is to have students generate and solve problems with real-world data. Put students in groups of three or four and give each group a copy of Skating Off the Snack (p. 49) and a calculator. You may wish to make an overhead transparency to use during the lesson.

Get going. Allow time for the students to read and discuss the material before proceeding. Pose and answer questions to help the students focus on the activity.

How many calories per minute will Pat burn up? How did you get that?

Will Jerry use more or fewer calories per minute than Pat? Why? Who will use the fewest? How did you decide that?

Whose lunch had the most calories? What could Pat have for lunch that could be skated off in about half an hour?

Can you select a lunch that would be about 1000 calories?

When the students are familiar with the data, suggest that they write other problems. When they have done so, assign the children to groups of four and suggest that they exchange papers with another group and attempt to solve the new problems.

Keep going. The activity is easily extended by using other lunch selections and sports or by varying the weights. Have the students consult a variety of sources to find out the number of calories used in various physical activities. Cookbooks are a resource for calorie charts.

This activity introduces students to the health concepts that calories taken in provide energy for the body and that each type of food has a caloric value. The study of calories and energy relates this mathematical lesson to physics, biology, and chemistry.

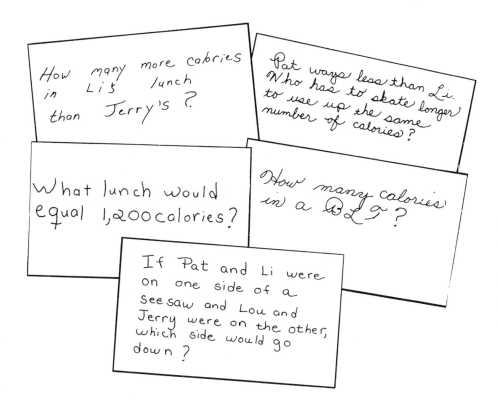

This is an appropriate time to lead class discussions about weight, mass, and gravity. If a kilogram scale is available, have the students weigh themselves, decide on a menu, and compute how long they would need to skate to burn off the calories in their snack.

Ask the groups to pose additional problems, discuss solution strategies, solve the problems, and write them on file cards. Collect the cards and share them with another classroom. You might contact a teacher in another school and have the students exchange the problems with that teacher's class by mail or by computer network.

HOW MANY BLADES OF GRASS ARE THERE?

Get ready. The purpose of this activity is to show students that sampling, measuring, averaging, and rounding add to a person's understanding of the large numbers used in the world around us.

An acre of good lawn contains about 564 536 500 blades of grass.

Many children and adults have no idea how much a million is, let alone a billion. This activity helps give meaning to such outlandishly large numbers.

You will need a small sampling square for each student. Have the students make their squares by cutting a hole 1 centimeter on a side from the center of a 3" x 5" file card. A trundle wheel or a measuring tape is also needed for this activity.

Get going. Explain to the class that they will collect information to help them estimate how many blades of grass there are in the school lawn or field. Send the students outdoors to count the number of blades of grass that can be seen through the hole in their index card when the card is placed on the lawn.

Questions are apt to arise: "Should we count the dead grass?" and "What's a blade?" Have each student report the number of blades of grass found.

Assign two students to measure the dimensions of the lawn by using the trundle wheel or the measuring tape. Round the lawn's dimensions to the nearest meter, then find its area.

Challenge the class to figure out how to use the information they have gathered to find the total number of blades of grass. Discuss possible strategies. Provide ample time for the students to explain and justify the solution to the problem. Lead them to compute the number of centimeter squares needed to fill the lawn. Multiply the class average by the number of square centimeters needed to cover the lawn to get a good estimate of the number of blades of grass in the designated area.

Keep going. This activity can be linked to a social studies unit or to a current event heard on a national news broadcast. How large is the national debt? How large a lawn area would we need to have enough blades of grass to represent the national debt? How long would it take to mow a lawn of that size? How much would the clippings weigh? After discussing these and similar questions, the students will have a better understanding of large numbers.

The question of satisfactory sampling should be raised. Did every blade have an equal opportunity to be counted? Probably not. If you send a group of students out to do this job, they usually bunch around each other and do not spread out over the lawn. This furnishes an excellent opportunity to talk about sampling errors. Should you count dead grass? What is a blade? These and similar questions provide a chance to clarify important concerns.

In 1992 the national debt was about four trillion dollars. How many rooms the size of the classroom would be needed to store the national debt if it were paid in one-dollar bills?

NUMBER DETECTIVE

Get ready. The purpose of this activity is to have students use reasoning skills in a number line context. The activity involves the recognition of the relationships between numbers and can focus on whole numbers, fractions, or decimals as appropriate to your class.

Give each student a copy of the Number Detective worksheet (p. 50) and several long, narrow strips of paper. You may wish to make an overhead transparency of the worksheet.

If students are to become mathematically powerful, they must be flexible enough to approach situations in a variety of ways and recognize the relationships among different points of view. (NCTM 1989a, p. 84)

Get going. Tell the students that they are detectives who must discover what number should be put in the boxes on each number line. Suggest that folding the paper strips may give them clues to what the number should be. Encourage them to use previously completed examples as they solve each new "mystery." When the students have finished, call on several of them to explain how they knew what number was indicated by the box. Encourage them to use proportional thinking as they explain their answers. (Example: The first box in the second line had to be 1/10 of 50 because 10 is 1/10 of 100.)

Keep going. Draw additional arrows and boxes on your transparency copy of the Number Detective. Select students to fill in the appropriate number and justify their decisions to the class.

Encourage the students to work in pairs. One student draws a line segment of any length, selects and labels the "endpoints," and indicates the placement of boxes; the other student fills in the missing numbers.

Feedback to students can have a variety of forms, including written or oral comments or numerical scores on a specific exercise. (NCTM 1989a, p. 209)

Students' mathematical dispositions are manifested in the way they approach tasks—whether with confidence, willingness to explore alternatives, perseverance, and interest—and in their tendency to reflect on their own thinking. (NCTM 1989a, p. 233)

This activity helps children see the many ways numbers can be formed. The flexibility of representing numbers in many ways is often called on in problem solving and in computation.

TARGET PRACTICE

Get ready. The purpose of this activity is to have students use mental arithmetic.

Prepare three number cubes with numbers on their faces as follows:

cube 1: 0, 1, 2, 3, 4, 5

cube 2: 6, 7, 8, 9, 1, 0

cube 3: 10, 10, 10, 1, 1, 1

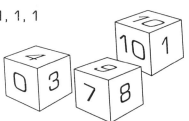

Get going. Have a student write down a number less than 100, toss the three cubes, and attempt to make an equation that results in the target number by using the three numbers showing "up" on the cubes. Allow any operations to be used. The student who comes closest to the target number wins.

Keep going. You may wish to use more cubes or to make some of the faces decimals or fractions.

Divide the class into teams. Throw the number cubes and record the results on the board. Class members have three minutes to write down as many mathematical sentences as they can, using these numbers. When time is called, team 1 reads their sentences. If anyone on team 2 has that sentence, both teams cross it off. Any sentence not crossed off (i.e., obtained by only one team) results in a point for that team. The first team to reach a designated score wins. For example, 2, 6, and 10 are recorded on the board. Here are just a few possible answers:

$$2 + 6 + 10 = 18$$
$$2 \times 6 + 10 = 22$$
$$6 \div 2 + 10 = 13$$

A variation of Target Practice is the game Decade. Use a regular deck of playing cards, allowing the ace to be 1 and removing the face cards. Players choose a target decade (i.e., 20, 30, 40) between 10 and 100. Each player draws four cards and uses any operation to try to come closest to the target decade. A player must use all four numbers drawn. Players could work as a team and plan together.

Target decade is 30:

$$6 \times 4 + 3 + A$$

SKATING OFF THE SNACK

Fact: Figure skating uses up about 1 calorie a minute for each 5 kilograms of body weight.

Skater	Weight	Lunch
Pat	50 kg	BLT (2 slices of bacon, 2 leaves of lettuce, 2 slices of tomato, mayo), banana
Lou	78 kg	2 hot dogs on rolls, apple
Jerry	40 kg	hamburger on a roll, orange, apple
Li	62 kg	hamburger on a roll, banana, slice of apple pie

Calorie Chart

Food	Amount	Calories
Broiled hamburger	4 oz.	180
Broiled hot dog	1	170
Roll	1	115
Bacon	2 slices	100
Lettuce	2 leaves	10
Tomato	1 slice	5
Bread	2 slices	140
Banana	1	100
Apple	1	100
Orange, large	1	95
Mayonnaise	1 T	110
Apple pie	1 slice	405

NUMBER DETECTIVE

Each number line segment has one or more arrows pointing to a specific spot on that number line. Below each arrow is a box. Write in the box the number that corresponds to the arrow's position on the number line.

Name _____

0   50   □   100

0   □   □   10

0   □   □

100   □   □   300

1   □   □   3

0   □   □   500

0   □   □   50

0   □   □   5

0   □   □   0 5

CHAPTER 7
SIXTH GRADE

For sixth graders, number sense is a critical component of their mathematics. Encouraging them to estimate and check answers as an integral part of any numerical exercise, discussing common measurement situations with them, and asking them to justify their mathematical choices will help these students develop this crucial ability.

Instruction that facilitates students' understanding of the underlying structure of arithmetic should employ informal explorations and emphasize the reasons why various kinds of numbers occur, commonalities among various arithmetic processes, and relationships between number systems. (NCTM 1989a, p. 91)

What could you measure with—

Millimeters?   Inches?   Miles?
piano keys   My foot   DISTANCE TO GRANDMA'S
FILM   the desk   Distance to the moon
                My cat's tail

Feet?   Kilometers?

MY BED   Distance to Tommy's house
Width of classroom rug How FAR THE SCHOOL BUS GOES

THE WORLD AROUND US

Get ready. The purpose of this activity is to have students practice estimating, ordering large numbers, and finding percentages with real-world data. The students' social studies teacher may wish to work with you in presenting this activity.

Get going. Give pairs of students maps of the world, transparent centimeter grids, and a list of countries belonging to the United Nations. Together, select five countries to study. Have each pair locate the first designated country on the map. Using the map's scale and the centimeter grid, the students should estimate each country's area.

Students' ability to reason, solve problems, and use mathematics to communicate their ideas will develop only if they actively and frequently engage in these processes. (NCTM 1989a, p. 244)

When the students have completed the task, find the class average and then consult a social studies textbook or other resource materials to see whether individual estimates or the average estimate is closer to the published figures. Repeat the activity to estimate the areas of the other four countries. Then ask the students to order the countries by area, using < and > signs. Encourage them to express the area in various ways, for example, 3 400 000 square kilometers or 3.4 million square kilometers.

Have the students select another country, find it on their maps and, on the basis of their previous work, write down their estimates of its area.

Encourage class discussion by asking questions such as these:

Peter, how did you arrive at your estimate? Did anyone else use a different strategy? Show us how you did it.

Can you find a country about the same size as India? Portugal? Chile? Malaysia?

On the basis of what you have observed, how large do you think Europe is?

Keep going. Have the students use several years of population figures, obtained from such library reference materials as the *World Almanac,* to estimate a country's population for some year in the future, say, the year 2000. After this research has been completed, have each team use calculators to compute the estimated growth rate for each country.

The data below may be used to help the class as a group practice finding projected growth rates.

Country	Population 1989	Projected population 2000
U.S.A	248 800 000	268 100 000
China	1 103 900 000	1 255 700 000
France	56 100 000	57 100 000
Canada	26 300 000	29 400 000
South Africa	38 500 000	46 900 000

Source: *World Almanac 1990*

China's Growth Rate

$$1,255,700,000$$
$$\underline{1,103,900,000}$$
$$151,800,000$$

$$\frac{151,800,000}{1,103,900,000} = 0.1374$$
or
$$13.7\%$$

Assign the children to groups of four and give them the task of finding the population density of several countries of their choice by using the data they have obtained (the area of a country in square units and its population).

Give each pair of students a copy of a world map and ask them to choose a country, cut it out of the map, and mount it on construction paper to make a poster. Have them write beside the country its current population, the population growth rate, and the expected population in the year 2000. They may wish to look up the area of the country and compute the current population density and the projected population density. Depending on what is currently being discussed in social studies class, other data might also be entered on the poster.

As a writing assignment, ask the students to project and discuss what problems caused by the increased population density could arise by the year 2000.

GOING SHOPPING

Get ready. The purpose of this activity is to have students create and solve word problems by using real-world data.

Calculators should be available for student use. Bring in newspaper advertisements or furnish students with an enlarged copy of the chart below.

Summer Sporting Equipment	
Item	Cost
Skateboard	$ 96.59
Skateboard wheels	23.50 (set)
Skateboard knee pads	6.25 (pair)
Skateboard arm guards	8.95 (pair)
Surfboard	181.50
Boogie board	79.95
Goggles	17.50
Wet suit	124.99

Get going. Ask each student to write a story problem, using the data provided. Encourage them to be creative both in setting up the situation and in choosing the type of mathematical procedures required to solve the problem. When they have finished, have them exchange papers and attempt to solve the problem they receive.

As the students attempt to solve the problems, they may discover that further clarification and revisions are needed. Provide time for editing. Partners should communicate with each other, edit the problems as necessary, and solve them.

After an appropriate period, call on students to read the edited problems and discuss the process they used to find the solution. Having other class members suggest alternative strategies will enrich this activity for all your students. To strengthen problem-posing skills, repeat the activity.

Let the students write the problems using a computer and word processing software. If computers are not available, the students can create a story file by writing their problems on 4 x 6 index cards. Have them sort the problems into different categories: levels of difficulty, number of steps required to solve, and operations used. The sorting activity will give you insight into the kinds of problems the students are

Data bases and computer programs can engage students in posing and solving problems. (NCTM 1989a, p. 76)

comfortable solving, the complexity of some students' work, and their sorting schemes. This information will help you better plan your mathematics lessons and learn more about each student in your class.

An interesting writing assignment for students' mathematics journals would be to have the students answer the following questions:

What kinds of problems are difficult to solve?

What makes a problem hard?

How can you tell when a problem is easy?

Keep going. You may wish to have students generate and share original problems based on similar data found in catalogs, menus, flyers, or newspaper ads. The problems can be shared by mail or by computer networking with other sixth graders. This activity will provide many opportunities for problem posing, editing, and solving.

BEAN CITY

Get ready. The purpose of this activity is to have students work with a situation that involves problem solving, estimating, and working with ratios.

Have available an assortment of weighing and measuring devices, then distribute to each group of four to six students an opaque bag filled with 1000 beans of mixed variety. Navy beans, pinto beans, and lima beans work well. Each group also needs one copy of the Bean City Census planning sheet (p. 56).

Get going. Tell the students that they are to act as census takers to determine the proportion of each kind of bean in Bean City, a small town with a population of 1000. However, they must sample the population, since the city council of Bean City is not willing to pay for a door-to-door census (an exact count). Guide the students in planning a sampling strategy.

You may wish to have a student list all the sampling suggestions on an overhead transparency or on the chalkboard. Discuss some of the suggested sampling procedures with the students and encourage them to carry out a variety of them using their beans. If the students do not suggest weighing as a possibility, prompt them to include this as a strategy.

As the students decide on a strategy and begin working on the Bean City census, suggest that they assign the job of scribe to one of their members. It will be the scribe's responsibility to document the results of the group's discussions, record the way they carry out their sampling procedure, and fill in the planning sheet.

Keep going. As groups complete their census, have them briefly discuss their estimates. Allow them to count the beans and to compare their estimates with the count. Briefly report the results from each group and have the students comment on which sampling strategies seemed to give the most accurate picture of the bean population. You will want to encourage the students to reflect on what happened in each group.

A bulletin board devoted to this activity will encourage the students to depict their data in several ways. Some students could write "newspaper" articles for the bulletin board; others could write editorials about the efficiency of different sampling techniques or write advertisements for different survey companies.

FIND IT FAST

Get ready. The purpose of this activity is to have students sharpen their ability to find percentages mentally.

Get going. Write on an overhead transparency or on the chalkboard the following percentage expressions, one at a time:

50 percent of 30;	10 percent of 12
20 percent of 50;	150 percent of 40
17 percent of 10;	13 percent of 10
40 percent of 75;	35 percent of 20
16 percent of 25;	62 percent of 50
125 percent of 40;	30 percent of 50

Ask the students to generate a quick way to compute the answer and to explain why the shortcut works.

Keep going. Encourage the students to generate percentage exercises that can be solved mentally and to share them with their classmates at the beginning or the end of class.

This Bean City activity creates a need for students to use ratios and is a logical introduction to the topic.

Bean City Samples

Sample	Navy	Pinto	Lima
A	3	5	2
B	4	8	3
C	2	6	1

Estimate of navy beans:

$9/34 = ?/1000$

$? = 9000/34$ navy beans

Overheard in the class:
Tomeka said, "Just take half for 50 percent."
Mary said, "I take 10 percent of 17 instead of 17 percent of 10."
Marea said, "If it is over 100 percent, I know the answer is greater than what I started with."
Jose said, "I use fractional equivalents whenever I can. If I want 25 percent of 16, I take 1/4 of 16."

BEAN CITY CENSUS

Census takers: _____ _____ _____ _____

There are 1000 beans in Bean City. Each bean belongs to one of these families: Navy, Pinto, or Lima. As a census taker, you need to plan how you will find out how many beans belong to each family. Describe your plan and carry it out.

Our Plan

Carry out your plan. Use the work space.

Work Space

Predictions

Number of Beans:

Pinto _____

Lima _____

Navy _____